*About the Marine Sanctuaries Conservation Series*

*The National Oceanic and Atmospheric Administration's National Ocean Service (NOS) administers the Office of National Marine Sanctuaries (ONMS). Its mission is to identify, designate, protect and manage the ecological, recreational, research, educational, historical, and aesthetic resources and qualities of nationally significant coastal and marine areas. The existing marine sanctuaries differ widely in their natural and historical resources and include nearshore and open ocean areas ranging in size from less than one to over 5,000 square miles. Protected habitats include rocky coasts, kelp forests, coral reefs, sea grass beds, estuarine habitats, hard and soft bottom habitats, segments of whale migration routes, and shipwrecks.*

*Because of considerable differences in settings, resources, and threats, each marine sanctuary has a tailored management plan. Conservation, education, research, monitoring and enforcement programs vary accordingly. The integration of these programs is fundamental to marine protected area management. The Marine Sanctuaries Conservation Series reflects and supports this integration by providing a forum for publication and discussion of the complex issues currently facing the sanctuary system. Topics of published reports vary substantially and may include descriptions of educational programs, discussions on resource management issues, and results of scientific research and monitoring projects. The series facilitates integration of natural sciences, socioeconomic and cultural sciences, education, and policy development to accomplish the diverse needs of NOAA's resource protection mandate. All publications are available on the Office of National Marine Sanctuaries Web site (http://www.sanctuaries.noaa.gov).*

# Office of National Marine Sanctuaries
# Science Review of Artificial Reefs

Kathy Broughton
NOAA Office of National Marine Sanctuaries

U.S. Department of Commerce
Rebecca Blank, Acting Secretary

National Ocean and Atmospheric Administration
Jane Lubchenco, Ph.D.
Under Secretary of Commerce for Oceans and Atmosphere

National Ocean Service
David M. Kennedy, Assistant Administrator

Office of National Marine Sanctuaries
Daniel J. Basta, Director

Silver Spring, Maryland
August 2012

## Disclaimer

Report content does not necessarily reflect the views and policies of the Office of National Marine Sanctuaries or the National Oceanic and Atmospheric Administration, nor does the mention of trade names or commercial products constitute endorsement or recommendation for use.

## Report Availability

Electronic copies of this report may be downloaded from the Office of National Marine Sanctuaries web site at http://sanctuaries.noaa.gov.

## Cover

The U.S.S. *Spiegel Grove* was scuttled as an artificial reef in 2002 in the Florida Keys National Marine Sanctuary. Photo courtesy of elmark.net.

## Suggested Citation

Broughton, K. 2012. Office of National Marine Sanctuaries Science Review of Artificial Reefs. Marine Sanctuaries Conservation Series ONMS-12-05. U.S. Department of Commerce, National Oceanic and Atmospheric Administration, Office of National Marine Sanctuaries, Silver Spring, MD. 42pp.

## Contact

Kathy Broughton
NOAA Office of National Marine Sanctuaries
1305 East West Highway
Silver Spring, MD 20910
Kathy.Broughton@noaa.gov
301-713-3125

# Table of Contents

# Overview

Artificial reefs are human-made structures that are either deliberately or unintentionally submerged underwater, commonly with the result of mimicking some characteristics of a natural reef. Artificial reefs alter local habitat by providing hard substrate and complex vertical relief where typically none previously existed (Bohnsack and Sutherland 1985, Sheehy and Vik 1992, Sheehy and Vik 2010). They may be created from a variety of sources and materials including the intentional sinking of ships and barges, rubble, concrete, rocks, stone, boulders, steel, and metal, etc. (Baine 2001). They may also be created through unintentional means (e.g., shipwrecks that can become historical in nature) and through structures built for other purposes (e.g., decommissioned oil and gas platforms, breakwaters[1], jetties, bridges, offshore lighthouses, air force towers, navigational aids, marine data buoys, etc.). These various materials have benefits and drawbacks when used in artificial reef construction (see Table 1 for examples).

The establishment of an artificial structure influences the surrounding underwater ecosystem by creating new habitat that can potentially change the abundance and distribution of living resources. Artificial structures can provide similar ecological functions as natural habitat, including developing epibiotic communities that create microhabitat for motile species, locally concentrate planktonic and pelagic food resources, alter current flows to provide sheltered areas, provide visual reference points, and create spawning sites (Bohnsack and Sutherland 1985, Sheehy and Vik 2010). Because of their ability to create habitat for a variety of marine life they are often popular destinations for divers, snorkelers, and fishermen. Therefore, their creation can also alter human use by shifting recreational diving and fishing patterns (Leeworthy et al. 2006, Leeworthy 2011).

General agreement exists in the scientific community that artificial reefs can effectively accumulate fish and other organisms (Bohnsack and Sutherland 1985). Somewhat less understood are the effects of artificial reefs on living resource production, their ability to act as stepping-stones that facilitate native and non-native species dispersal, how they affect disease frequency in fish and invertebrates, toxicological impacts, their long-term structural integrity, and changes to the socioeconomic conditions of adjacent coastal communities. The purpose of this paper is to summarize the scientific literature and findings on these subjects.

---

[1]  Submerged breakwaters as a means of shoreline stabilization, coastal erosion mitigation, and enhancement of local surfing conditions are also sometimes referred to as "artificial reefs." These structures have received increased attention in recent years (ESA PWA 2012); however, because they are not intentionally deployed in marine environments to perform habitat-enhancing roles, discussion of artificial reefs as shoreline protective devices is beyond the scope of this document.

**Table 1. Comparison of various materials that have been used in the development of underwater artificial reefs in the United States. Although used historically, material types in shaded rows are currently prohibited for use as artificial reefs by the U.S. Army Corps of Engineers due to past negative performance (*Source: modified from AGSMFC 2004*).**

| Material Type | Benefits | Drawbacks |
|---|---|---|
| Concrete, secondary use materials (culverts, storm water junction boxes, etc.) | Cost effective; material is compatible with marine environment; material is highly durable and stable; readily available; can be cast into many forms; provides surfaces for settlement and growth of encrusting organisms. | Heavy weight; higher cost needed for deployment. Waterfront staging area is needed for long term accumulation of donated materials. |
| Steel Hulled Vessels | Make for interesting diving locations and as such can generate economic contributions to coastal communities; durable at certain depths; attract both pelagic and demersal fishes; provide surface area for epibenthic colonization. | Stability during hurricanes is variable; durability can be compromised due to salvage; removal of hazardous materials is expensive. |
| Oil and Gas Platforms | Provide habitat for a variety of species; durable and stable; readily available. | Could pose obstructions to navigation; expensive to move or remove structures; potential to attract invasive species. |
| Concrete designed structures | Can be engineered to address specific goals and objectives of an artificial reef program; standardized modules provide valuable opportunities for research monitoring; can be readily available if vendors are local; long-term stability. | Can be limiting due to lack of funding and module manufacturers; deployment can be more expensive in comparison to secondary use materials. |
| Natural materials (e.g., rock, shell) | Can be readily available. | Excavation of natural materials may have terrestrial environmental trade-offs. |
| Automobiles | Readily available; easy to handle. | Require a great deal of preparation prior to deployment; not durable or stable. |
| Tires | Easy to handle; readily available; low cost; long life-span. | Leaching of petrochemical or heavy metal toxicants is possible; un-ballasted tires are unstable; properly ballasted tired are more expensive and difficult to handle. |
| Wood | Can be readily available. | Short-term stability and life span. |

## Attraction Versus Production

Artificial reefs have been purposely deployed in coastal and offshore habitats, including some national marine sanctuaries, to enhance the production of reef-associated species (e.g., macroalgae, invertebrates, and fish). Often, this increased production has historically been aimed to mitigate the losses from overfishing and other anthropogenic pressures (e.g., pollution, habitat destruction, etc.). For example, in Thunder Bay within Lake Huron artificial reefs have been established to mitigate aquatic habitat degradation and loss that has resulted from cement kiln dust deposition (a waste by-product of cement production) by creating approximately two acres of new habitat for spawning fishes. Artificial reefs are also created to enhance the convenience and efficiency of fishing for reef-associated species, which in turn may reduce fishing pressure on natural reefs (Ambrose 1994, Carr and Hixon 1997). More recently, engineering more difficult to detect small low-profile reefs and developing reefs aimed at reducing fishing pressure at natural sites have been implemented with greater emphasis to integrate artificial reef construction with fisheries management objectives. Today, critical questions during the planning process include contemplation of the impacts that artificial structures have on living resource production. For example, perhaps the most commonly asked question with regards to artificial reef development is if they primarily increase fish production or aggregate fish. The production hypothesis suggests that reef habitat is a limiting factor and that artificial reefs increase fish production by providing a habitat that would otherwise not be present. The attraction hypothesis proposes that fish are simply attracted to artificial reefs, and questions whether fishes that recruit to artificial reefs could have instead recruited to natural reefs. If so, do artificial reefs impact growth, mortality, and emigration (Carr and Hixon 1997)?

Attraction is the net movement of individual organisms from natural to artificial habitats (Carr and Hixon 1997). Production, somewhat more difficult to observe, is best quantified as a change in biomass through time. It reflects births, immigration, growth, death, and emigration (Carr and Hixon 1997). Several scientists and research managers have addressed the attraction-production issue in research and literature, but the relative levels of each, and the factors affecting them, have yet to be unequivocally resolved (Bohnsack and Sutherland 1985, Bohnsack 1989, Bohnsack et al. 1991, Bohnsack et al. 1997, Lindberg 1997, Herrnkind et al. 1997, Grossman et al. 1997). As a result, today it is widely acknowledged that artificial reefs function both in attraction and production. Some findings suggest that artificial reefs allow for secondary biomass production through increased survival and growth of new individuals by providing additional food sources; shelter from predation and shelf currents; a point of physical orientation; increased recruitment habitat for settling individuals that would otherwise be lost to the population; and vacated space in the natural environment that allows replacement from outside the system (Randall 1963, Bohnsack and Sutherland 1985, Bohnsack 1989, Meier et al. 1989, Carr and Hixon 1997, Love et al. 2006, Otake and Oshitani 2006, REEF 2007, Shipp and Bortone 2009). Other study results suggest that by aggregating existing scattered individuals, artificial reefs can have deleterious effects on exploited populations by making remaining fish too easy to catch, especially if overfishing is a problem (Bohnsack 1989, Meier et al. 1989, Grossman et al. 1997). Concentrated fishing effort and catch at artificial reefs can increase the potential for over exploitation. In addition, recent analysis of natural mortality and fishing mortality estimates show the overwhelming influence fishing pressure has on fish stocks, regardless of the presence of artificial reefs (Patterson et al. 2009). One component of mortality related to fishing is a result of release mortality caused by barotrauma and/or hook injuries. Recent efforts towards reducing release mortality include implementation of de-hooking and venting tools, recompression devices, and circle hooks. By giving consideration towards placement of artificial reefs intended for fishing opportunities at depth locations to minimize barotraumas injuries artificial reefs could potentially play a role towards the effort to reduce release mortality. Thus, artificial reef design and fisheries management on artificial reefs, both under the authority of resource managers, may influence the levels of attraction and production (Pickering and Whitmarsh 1996).

Studies have shown that the materials and design of artificial reefs impact their relative value as a fisheries enhancement tool. Historically, most artificial reefs consisted of manufactured materials (see Table 1), such as metal or concrete. Studies have shown higher species abundance with increasing structural volume and complexity of artificial reefs (Potts and Hulbert 1994, Spieler et al. 2001, Quinn 2009) with larger, more structurally complex reefs (e.g., structures with holes, overhangs, and shadows) providing more opportunity for animals to recruit and thus may lead to a higher local biological diversity (Menge 1976). Brock and Norris (1989) compared four artificial reef designs and found that reefs composed of haphazardly dumped scrap materials (automobile shells and surplus concrete pipe) provided the poorest enhancement, while reefs composed of modules of scrap automobile tires set in concrete bases and dumped haphazardly showed moderate enhancement that varied with the degree of module dispersion. Significantly greater enhancement effects (e.g., mean standing crop, mean size per fish and mean number of species) were attained on an artificial reef constructed in an open framework of concrete cube modules that were arranged to provide maximum refuge space for fishes. Their data suggest that haphazard deployment of materials provided significantly poorer enhancement relative to a reef constructed of designed modules assembled into a specific configuration.

Carr and Hixon (1997) suggested that placement of artificial reefs also largely determines how much attraction and/or production occur. They presented three possible scenarios that were tested in field studies. In the first, they concluded that a management area with only an artificial reef would increase regional production. In the second scenario, a management area included an artificial reef located offshore from a natural reef with a strong long shore current present. They concluded that the current would preclude larval or migratory transport between the natural reef and the artificial reef and that if the artificial reef did not exist, the larvae that settled on it would be lost from the management area. That artificial reef, therefore, would increase production in the management area. In the final scenario, an artificial reef was located up current from a natural reef in a management area. They concluded that attraction dominated in this case because intercepted larvae grew less well on the artificial reef than they would have on a natural reef. Total growth and production would have been higher if the larvae intercepted by the artificial reef could have settled on a natural reef. A more recent study by Love et al. (2007) further examined this premise. Their examination of daily growth rates of young-of-the-year (YOY) blue rockfish (*Sebastes mystinus*), through parings from natural and artificial reefs, demonstrated that juvenile blue rockfish living at the artificial habitat of oil and gas production platforms grew at least as well as those at natural reefs, and in one case grew more productively than those at natural reefs. By Carr and Hixon's definition, production is occurring from these artificial habitats and Love et al.'s results further imply that some artificial reefs may benefit regional fish populations.

Another study by Emery et al. (2006) further supported the potential importance of artificial reefs in larval recruitment. Results from this oceanic current study indicate that most of the YOY bocaccio (*Sebastes paucispinis*; a species of concern as determined by NOAA National Marine Fisheries Service, and a fishery stock determined to be depleted and overfished by the Pacific Fishery Management Council) that settled around Platform Irene (located west of Point Conception, California) during two separate years would not have survived in the absence of the platform. Instead, prevailing currents would likely advect the YOY's offshore where they would have a very low probability of survival. Although it is possible that some individuals would encounter acceptable nursery habitat on offshore banks or islands, it is likely that most would perish. This study demonstrated that the presence of Platform Irene almost certainly increases the survival of YOY bocaccio in the Point Conception–Point Arguello region off California. Further, the study also shows that knowledge of regional ocean circulation patterns is essential for evaluating the effects of oil production platforms or other artificial habitats on dispersal pathways. Location of artificial habitat, oceanographic current patterns and presence/absence of suitable natural habitat and its distribution determine the balance between settlement on an artificial reef and settlement on natural habitat.

Further complicating the attraction-production issue is the question of whether the communities that form at artificial reef sites mimic natural reef communities. Many studies have shown that artificial reefs have a higher abundance and biomass than randomly selected bottom control areas, however, natural and artificial reefs generally have similar fish community structure (see Bohnsack and Sutherland 1985). It has been found that the structural complexity provided by artificial reefs contributes to the greater density of fishes on artificial reefs in comparison to natural reefs (Smith et al. 1979, Bohnsack et al. 1994, Eklund 1996). As an example, a study by Walton (1982) found that the density of fish on artificial reefs was eight times greater in comparison to natural reefs. In addition, a study in the Gulf of Mexico demonstrated that the deployment of thousands of petroleum platforms transformed the region from a relatively unproductive area for the habitat-limited red snapper to one of the most productive red snapper areas in the Gulf of Mexico (Shipp and Bartone 2009)[2]. However, it should be noted that in most cases (particularly areas with relatively fewer artificial reefs) although fish density is usually higher on artificial reefs than natural reefs, the actual total abundance of fishes on artificial reefs can be trivial compared to natural reefs because most artificial reefs cover

---

[2] It should be noted that Cowan et al. 2010 discounts this study because they contend Shipp and Bartone provide little information on red snapper life history or ecology, nor do they provide a mechanistic explanation for the thesis that artificial reefs have increased red snapper stock-specific productivity.

a much smaller total area. Therefore, in these instances, the contribution of artificial reefs to total fish abundance is trivial (DeMartini et al. 1989).

A key issue is habitat limitation and whether or not artificial reefs provide critical habitat for increased production that would not otherwise be possible. Reef fish abundance has traditionally been considered limited by habitat or space partly because reefs are a patchy resource, limited in geographical coverage and separated from other reefs (Bohnsack 1989). Habitat can be limiting primarily by the availability of food or shelter from predation (Bohnsack 1989). Studies have shown that the transformation of low-relief habitats (e.g., predominantly sandy mud habitats) to one having increased areas of high relief (and hard bottom) can increase fish abundance (Shipp 1999, Osenberg et al. 2002, Shipp and Bortone 2009). Bortone (2008) presented a model that demonstrates that not only do artificial reefs attract fish but, in addition, they may also provide increased habitat that relieves a "bottleneck" in the life history that previously restricted population abundance. However, some fishery scientists argue that habitat is not limiting (Lindberg 1997, Cowan et al. 2010, Lindberg et al. 2006). One reasoning is that before reef fishes were heavily exploited, the existing natural habitat supported an abundance of reef fish, presumably at or near carrying capacity. Fishing mortality later reduced stocks, yet the amount of natural habitat remained the same. With fish stocks substantially below carrying capacity, they reason that the amount of habitat could not be the factor that limits population size. An alternative is that instead most adult reef fish populations are limited by recruitment variability (Doherty and Williams 1998, Doherty and Fowler 1994, Booth and Brosnan 1995). In the cases of heavily exploited species with depleted populations, a lack of spawning adults may limit recruitment success and population replenishment. Some scientists note that some species are habitat-limited while others are recruitment-limited (Bohnsack et al. 1991). Results from a study by Lindberg et al. (2006) suggest that the attraction–production issue is a false dichotomy in that high densities of fish result from processes such as density-dependent habitat selection rather than behavioral artifacts, and that whether or not artificial reefs are ecological traps depends on associated fishing mortality.

The discussions surrounding artificial reefs need to evolve from the single issue of attraction versus production to an evaluation of the overall ecological performance of fishes at natural versus artificial reefs (Love et al. 2006), and how these dynamics change over time. Comparisons of natural versus artificial reefs should examine: 1) survival rate of young fishes at the two habitat types, 2) the density of recruiting juveniles at an artificial reef versus surrounding natural reefs, 3) the possibility that an artificial reef is attracting fishes from nearby natural reefs, and 4) the source of fishes found on an artificial reef (Love et al. 2006).

The above questions on the performance of artificial reefs are complex; one cannot be answered without considering the others.

## Range Expansion

Artificial structures may provide habitat that can directly or indirectly support recruitment and range expansion for various organisms including sponges, bryozoans, barnacles, hydroids, corals[3], and associated fish communities (Shinn 1974, Rooker et al. 1997, Sammarco et al. 2004, Atchison 2005, Love and York 2005, Sheehy and Vik 2010). Artificial structures provide hard substrate, which may increase the supply of prey, shelter, and spawning sites that could alter the local distributions of species and potentially contribute to range expansions (Rooker et al. 1997, Casell et al. 2002). Studies have shown that algae, invertebrates, and fishes are capable of colonizing new reef structures rapidly (Fager 1971, Bohnsack and Talbot 1980, Bohnsack and Sutherland 1985). As such, artificial structures, particularly offshore oil and gas platforms, have been described as potential stepping-stones for the expansion of various living resource communities. It should be noted that the majority of fish and invertebrate species that are observed on both artificial and natural reefs do not spend their entire life in these habitats. Different stages of development may have different habitat requirements and population limitations. For these reasons, organisms observed on an artificial structure are ecologically part of a number of interconnected populations. Therefore, an artificial structure can affect other populations across regions and habitats (Schroeder and Love 2004).

Studies have examined recruitment and succession on artificial reefs. Oil and gas platforms have been shown to support the expansion and growth of sessile invertebrate communities (Shinn 1974, Sammarco et al. 2004, Atchison 2005, Sheehy and Vik 2010). Much of the northern Gulf of Mexico region is characterized by mud substrate with low habitat diversity, thus making it unavailable to sessile, epibenthic hard bottom organisms. When oil and gas platforms were introduced in the Gulf of Mexico they provided additional hard structure for benthic colonization and represented one of the few shallow-water (less than 20 meters depth), hard substrate habitats in the region. Since the 1940s, approximately 7,000 oil and gas platforms have been installed in the Gulf of Mexico. Today there are approximately 3,300 oil and gas platforms in federal waters in the Gulf of Mexico (D. Peter, Louisiana Dept. of Wildlife and Fisheries Artificial Reef Program, pers. comm., 2011)[4]. One study estimated that the presence of about 3,800 oil and gas

---

[3] In an attempt to restore coral reefs by propagating coral species that have witnessed dramatic population declines due to stressors such as hurricanes and disease coral gardening techniques have been employed. Coral gardening consists of growing corals in-situ at a nursery site, and then transplanting these coral fragments back onto both natural and artificial reef environments once they have grown to an appropriate size. Coral gardening has been undertaken using varied methods of fragment or nubbin attachment such as mid-water wire frames, floating platforms, limestone, concrete, and suspended lines (Herlan and Lirman 2008). These structures are sometimes considered to be "artificial reefs;" however, because they are not intentionally deployed in marine environments to perform habitat-enhancing roles, discussion of coral gardening techniques is beyond the scope of this document.

[4] In the past, most decommissioned oil and gas platforms in the Gulf of Mexico have been removed and recycled. However, forty percent of these structures were single pile caissons, and not considered substantial structures for artificial reef use. Approximately 10% of all platforms have been "reefed" in designated artificial reef sites (see *Rigs-to-Reef* section). Occasionally platforms have been reinstalled and reused in other offshore locations and continue as petroleum production facilities.

platforms provided approximately 12 km$^2$ of additional hard substrate, or about a 0.4% increase in hardbottom habitat over naturally occurring reef (LGL Ecological Research Associates 1998). Primary benthic organisms associated with oil and gas platforms in the Gulf of Mexico include bivalve mollusks, barnacles, hydroids, and sponges. For example, a study of petroleum platforms near the Louisiana coast by Lewbel et al. (1987) found that the main habitat-forming species were barnacles and pelecypods, which accounted for over 99% of their samples.

Studies have shown that these platforms can also act as hard substrate upon which reef organisms can recruit and grow, including sessile algae, anemones, sponges, corals, and other attached organisms (Shinn 1974, Sammarco et al. 2004, Atchison 2005). Genetic analyses conducted by Atchison (2005) showed that oil and gas platforms facilitate the spread of coral larvae by acting as stepping stones where larvae that have been dispersed from the Flower Garden Banks or other natural reefs can settle and eventually spawn, thus dispersing corals further to additional platforms. Sammarco et al. (2004) found that oil and gas platforms are capable of supporting coral growth in areas where none previously existed, suggesting that they can extend species ranges. Their study also showed that many coral community variables are correlated with platform age, demonstrating that as the platforms age, coral abundance, species diversity, and colony size increase. As a result of these findings, the researchers determined that the oil and gas platforms in the Gulf of Mexico may provide beneficial environmental value with respect for some species of corals (Sammarco et al. 2004, Atchison 2005). However, it is important to note that the orange cup coral (*Tubastraea coccinea*), an invasive coral species, was one of the most abundant coral species observed in the Sammarco et al. (2004) study. In general, benthic communities that are found on platforms in the Gulf of Mexico are not representative of natural coral reef communities, but do contain some coral reef species (G. Schmahl, FGBNMS, pers. comm., 2012).

Artificial structures have also been shown to allow some species to increase their ranges into areas where they did not previously exist — a form of range extension referred to as "island hopping" (MacArthur and Wilson 1967, Pattengill 1998). Various environmental factors contribute to fish attraction to artificial reefs, including visual cues of size, shape, color, and light; sound; touch; and pressure (Bohnsack and Sutherland 1985). In addition, species type, fish age, season, and artificial reef age, structural characteristics, and location also influence recruitment rates (Bohnsack and Sutherland 1985). Pattengill (1998) proposed that the introduction of sergeant major (*Abudefduf saxatilis*) to the Flower Garden Banks was the result of "island hopping." Sergeant major, a species known to require shallow habitat for settlement, historically was absent from the Flower Garden Banks. However, she found that with the introduction of artificial shallow habitat (mooring lines and nearby oil and gas platforms), juvenile recruits were seen near the surface on these structures, and subsequently populations eventually became established. Rooker et al. (1997) also found reef fish expansion to have occurred at an oil platform in the Flower Garden Banks National Marine Sanctuary (HI-A389A, located in 125 m of water, and approximately 2 km and 22 km from the high diversity reef zones of East and West Banks, respectively). He found a similar faunal composition at the platform as on adjacent natural communities on East and West Flower Garden Banks, although higher numbers of species were observed on the natural reefs than on platforms due to greater habitat area available on the natural reefs.

Love and York (2005) conducted a study in southern California that compared fish assemblages of a platform and associated pipeline with that of the adjacent, natural seafloor. Their research strongly suggests that platforms, and their adjacent shell mounds, provide considerable hard substrate that can allow for fish range expansion by providing important habitat and nursery grounds for a variety of juvenile and diminutive fish species, particularly rockfishes (*Sebastes* spp.) and lingcod (*Ophiodon elongatus*). They found that many of the species that were found on the pipelines, particularly rockfish, were absent from the seafloor. They also found that the fish assemblages found on the pipelines were similar to those that occupy low-relief habitats such as cobble, small boulders, and shell mounds. The pipeline they studied appeared to also act as a nursery for a number of fishes, some of which (e.g., blackgill, flag, greenspotted, and splitnose rockfishes) recruit directly to the pipeline as young-of-the-year.

*Rigs-to-Reefs*

Offshore platforms, acting as artificial habitat, can play very different roles in ecosystem function. Platforms in the Gulf of Mexico are concentrated in the north-central and northwestern regions, where, in some cases, particularly in the nearshore and mid-shelf zones, natural reefs are not abundant, and as such they typically harbor unique communities that bear little resemblance to those in the natural surrounding habitat. It has been suggested if these platforms were to instead remain undisturbed their associated communities would be permitted to develop fully (Atchison 2005, Scarborough-Bull et al. 2008, OST 2010). In addition, it has been suggested that retired platforms would also provide recreational diving and fishing opportunities, and to a lesser extent, benefits to the commercial fishing community as well (OST 2010, Scarborough-Bull et al. 2008). A study by Scarborough-Bull et al. (2008) provides evidence that the artificial habitat supplied by the platforms in the Gulf of Mexico has increased the regional carrying capacity for economically important reef fish species such as red snapper (*Lutjanus campechanus*). Platforms in the Gulf of Mexico are customary destinations for both commercial and recreational fishing. Their study results showed that when the number of offshore platforms increased over decades, the production of reef fish also increased within the system and commercial fisheries for red snapper relocated to coincide with the geographic patterns of platform installation. In addition, recreational fisheries increased concomitantly with the increasing number of platforms.

Contrary to the Gulf of Mexico experience, California platforms are concentrated in the Santa Barbara Channel area among natural reefs and offshore islands. They typically harbor fish assemblages that resemble those found in nearby habitats. Off southern California, increased production of rockfish at platforms when compared to populations found on nearby natural reefs may be attributed, in part, to platform nursery function, larval production (Love et al. 2006), juvenile growth rates (Scarborough-Bull et al. 2008) and minimal fishing efforts at platforms. Observations by Scarborough-Bull et al. (2008) at natural reefs and platforms off California found that platforms have become harvest

10

refugia for increasingly rare and overfished species, which is thought to be a direct result of continual fishing pressure at natural reefs and a lack of fishing pressure at platforms. Significant differences in fishing pressure on natural versus artificial sites causes southern California platforms to act as de facto "no-take" marine protected areas. Thus, Scarborough-Bull et al.'s study demonstrates that there is a continuum along the full spectrum with attraction at one end and production at the other for any artificial reef or reef system and Rigs-to-Reefs are thought to increase and/or maintain production for a number of reef-related species in the Gulf of Mexico and in the southern California bight on local to regional scales.

The oil and gas industry is faced with hundreds of aging platforms that are approaching the end of their production capability. Estimates are that one thousand rigs in the Gulf of Mexico will be retired over the next decade (Salcido 2005) and 27[5] will be decommissioned in California's state tidelands and off the outer continental shelf (OST 2010). Federal legislation requires that all oil and gas platforms in U.S. waters must be removed within five years after they are considered to be no longer useful for operations (BOEM 2010). Cost estimates for the removal of a platform range from $50,000 for short platforms in very shallow waters to $15 million for tall platforms in the deepest waters (Salcido 2005). From 2000 to 2010 approximately 150 platforms were decommissioned each year (D. Peter, Louisiana Dept. of Wildlife and Fisheries Artificial Reef Program, pers. comm., 2011), thus causing the loss of hard substrate, which could reduce fish populations and encrusting organisms that depend on the hard substrate for survival.

For this reason, the Rigs-to-Reefs program, administered by the Bureau of Ocean Energy Management (BOEM, formerly part of the Minerals Management Service), was developed to permit platforms scheduled for decommissioning to either remain either on site or be brought to another site to be used as artificial reefs (Sammarco et al. 2004, Atchison 2005). The ownership and responsibility of the platform is then transferred to a public agency, which accepts title and responsibility for the structure as a permanent reef. Initially established in the 1980s, the program is funded by cost savings from this less expensive disposal option. Rigs-to-Reefs projects avoid some of the more costly decommissioning activities such as transportation, onshore dismantling, and payment of disposal fees (Salcido 2005). To date, 378 platforms in federal waters of the Gulf of Mexico have been reefed since 1973 (D. Peter, Louisiana Dept. of Wildlife and Fisheries Artificial Reef Program, pers. comm., 2011). Because a substantial number of the Gulf of Mexico platforms are scheduled to be decommissioned in the near future and hundreds of platforms and/or rigs were damaged or destroyed during hurricanes Rita and Katrina, there has been a recent increase in Rigs-to-Reefs applications (Sammarco et al. 2004, Sheehy and Vik 2010). The oil industry is a common proponent of the Rigs-to-Reefs program, simply because such a program reduces operating costs. Recreational fishermen and divers are also strong supporters of Rigs-to-Reefs because they believe artificial reefs

---

[5] An independent cost estimate for removal of the 27 federal platforms off California was completed for the Department of the Interior (Proserve Offshore 2010) which estimated that it would cost approximately $1.3 billion to remove the 27 platforms in federal waters. In addition, the review also shows that, in most cases, the cost of decommissioning continues to increase over time.

provide fishing and diving opportunities. Both groups also argue that decommissioning offshore platforms can have detrimental environmental impacts through air, water, and land pollution. In addition, habitat and marine life in the vicinity of the platforms is often lost to due to impacts from the large equipment and explosives that are required for their removal (OST 2010).

Conflicting opinions exist about the value of artificial reefs and the possible benefit that a Rigs-to-Reefs program could have on the marine environment. Critics argue that the goals of Rigs-to-Reef projects are more to subsidize oil production than improve fisheries, and as such, they reject these projects as ocean dumping rather than as an approach to enhance marine resources (Salcido 2005). It is also argued that artificial reef science is insufficiently developed and significant scientific uncertainty still remains in the attraction-versus-production debate, thus calling into question the value of converting a rig to a reef and having such a program be endorsed at a policy level. Groups such as the Ocean Conservancy and the Natural Resources Defense Council suggest considerably more evaluation of artificial reefs is necessary, and they point out that little restoration of failing marine health can be achieved by recreational use of artificial reefs (Salcido 2005). In addition, opponents also suggest that Rigs-to-Reefs programs also perpetuate the practice of ocean dumping of wastes. Some even go as far as to state that "these projects are nothing more than legally-approved garbage dumping that attracts fish away from valuable fisheries habitat" (Salcido 2005).

In California the government and industry are planning to decommission 27 offshore platforms (Salcido 2005, OST 2010) at an estimated cost of $1.09 billion for their complete removal (OST 2010). A Rigs-to-Reefs program was instituted in California in September 2010. The law (AB 2503) allows for the partial removal of a decommissioned oil platform as an alternative to complete removal, but only if the conversion would result in a net benefit to the marine environment. The bill also created the California Endowment for Marine Preservation, which receives the cost savings and uses it to fund marine protection projects and programs in perpetuity. Compared to the Gulf States, California has limited experience and infrastructure in decommissioning obsolete oil production facilities, and unlike the Gulf of Mexico, California stakeholder views are highly polarized. Therefore, it will be critical to define the social and ecological goals of these decommissioned platforms as artificial reefs. Studies by Schroeder and Love (2004) demonstrated that a pipeline in southern California (the Gail-Grace pipeline) is an important habitat and nursery ground for a number of juvenile and diminutive fish species, including some exploited species, such as cowcod, blackgill, and vermilion rockfishes. The extent of this significance as habitat will play an important role in determining preferred options in future decommissioning activities once oil production ceases (Schroeder and Love 2004).

## Invasive Species

Non-indigenous species are recognized worldwide as a major threat to ecosystem integrity if they become invasive. Non-indigenous species in the marine environment can alter community composition by competing with native species for food and space, reducing the abundance and diversity of native marine species, interfering with ecosystem function, introducing diseases, altering habitats, disrupting commercial and recreational activities, and in some instances causing extinction of indigenous plants and animals (Olden et al. 2004, Clavero and Garcia-Berthou 2005, Ruiz-Carus et al. 2006). Local extinction of native species can occur either via non-indigenous species preying on them directly or by out-competing them for food or space. Once established, non-indigenous species can be difficult, if not impossible, to control or eradicate.

Artificial structures may facilitate invasive species introductions and establishment by transporting attached fouling communities, providing new unoccupied habitat for establishment, and creating corridors for further dispersal and expansion (Glasby et al. 2007, Sheehy and Vik 2010, Figure 1). Invasions by non-indigenous aquatic species are increasingly common worldwide due to shipping traffic, world trade, and intentional or accidental releases of aquarium animal and plants. Though the most significant global mechanism for the introduction of aquatic species is ship ballast water, biofouling communities on ships or oil and gas platforms and the placement of human-made structures that provide new habitat are also identified as probable vectors for the spread of invasive species (Wasson et al. 2005, Glasby et al. 2007, Tyrrell and Byers 2007, Sheehy and Vik 2010). Artificial reefs with extensive vertical hard substrate provide large amounts of surface area, creating habitat for marine organisms, including invasive species. Because artificial reefs are often located in areas that lack hard bottom habitat, they typically provide unoccupied or novel substrate for colonization (Wasson et al. 2005, Tyrrell and Byers 2007, Sheehy and Vik 2010).

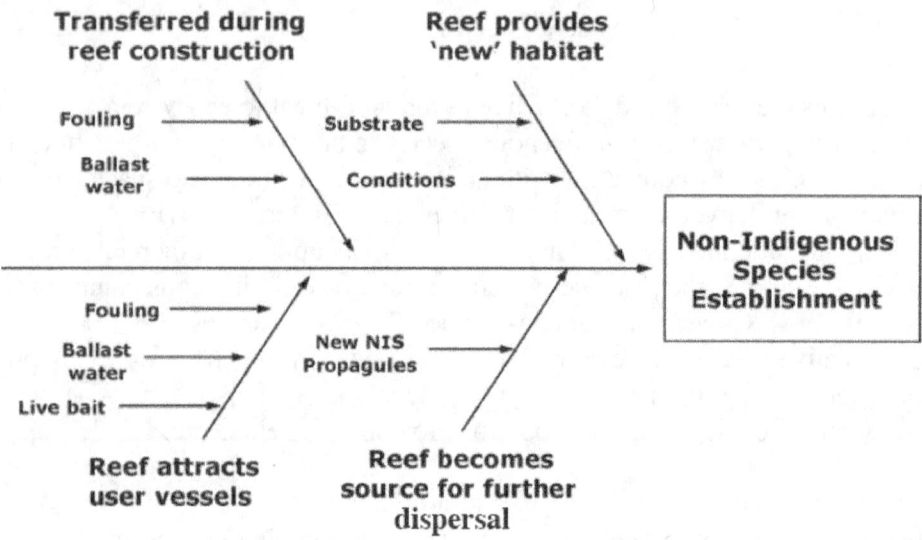

**Figure 1. Cause and effect diagram illustrating how constructing reefs may result in the establishment of non-indigenous species** (*Source: Sheehy and Vik 2010*).

Most studies on the role of artificial structures in facilitating marine invasions involve attached fouling organisms or invertebrates with relatively limited dispersal ability. Studies in Elkhorn Slough, an estuary in the Monterey Bay National Marine Sanctuary in Central California, have demonstrated that novel, hard artificial structures (e.g., pilings, gravel bars, jetties, rip-rap, docks) are much more heavily fouled by marine invertebrate invasive species in comparison to soft substrate (Wasson et al. 2005). Additional studies (Glasby et al. 2007, Tyrrell and Byers 2007) found greater numbers of nonindigenous epibiotic species than native species on artificial structures than on natural reefs. An explanation for the propensity for artificial, hard structures to attract invasive species in estuaries is that estuaries are typically dominated by soft sediments with the exception of oyster beds and driftwood. As such, there are few competitive, native, estuarine, sessile hard substratum species (Wasson et al. 2005). Also, because these structures are novel, there is no evolutionary history for native species on such surfaces (Wasson et al. 2005, Tyrrell and Byers 2007, Glasby et al. 2007).

In the Gulf of Mexico, invasive invertebrate species have been reported on artificial reefs and oil and gas platforms (Sammarco et al. 2004). They include the proliferation of coral (e.g., orange cup coral *Tubastraea coccinea*), two species of mussel (the brown mussel *Perna perna* and the green mussel *P. viridis*), a tunicate (*Didemnum perlucidum*), and jellyfish (Australian spotted jellyfish *Phyllorhiza punctata*).

As a case study, the orange cup coral (*Tubastraea coccinea*) (likely introduced in the 1940s), has now invaded the Gulf of Mexico, Brazil, and Florida (Fenner and Banks 2004, Ferry 2009, Shearer 2010). Observations in the Caribbean and the Gulf of Mexico show that this species can cause tissue necrosis and partial mortality of native corals (Creed 2006). It primarily appears on artificial substrates such as submerged steel wrecks and oil and gas platforms (Fenner and Banks 2004, Ferry 2009, Shearer 2010). It is suspected that in addition to dispersal vectors such as attachment to boats and drifting in currents, these artificial structures play a major role in the spread of this species (Fenner and Banks 2004). By 1999, *Tubastrea* sp. was commonly observed on Gulf of Mexico oil and gas platforms, located in federal waters off the coast of Texas (J. Embesi, FGBNMS, pers. comm., 2011). In 2002 the species was first documented on natural substrate at the East Flower Garden Bank, suggesting it had begun to invade the sanctuary, most likely from nearby oil and gas platforms (e.g., an active gas platform, HIA389A, located one mile from the reef cap of East Flower Garden Bank, has extensive colonies of orange cup corals) (Hickerson and Schmahl 2005). In 2011, orange cup coral was identified for the first time at the West Flower Garden Bank during monitoring surveys (E. Hickerson, FGBNMS, pers. comm., 2011). It has also been documented to be well established on Geyer and Sonnier Banks located in the northwestern Gulf of Mexico (Schmahl et al. 2008). A study by Ferry (2009) indicates that orange cup coral has not yet become established in the lower Florida Keys, but it is present in high abundance on the surfaces of the Aquarius underwater habitat off Key Largo in the upper Florida Keys. Large populations have also been reported on the U.S.C.G. *Duane* and U.S.S. *Spiegel Grove* (Shearer 2010). The potential for this species to impact reef communities in this region is high due to a lack of natural predators, high proliferation rates, and the ability to out-compete native species for limited available substrate.

Structural habitat is an important resource for mobile taxa like reef fishes as it provides refuge from predation, and reproduction and foraging sites. Few studies have examined whether artificial reef availability facilitates the introduction and establishment of invasive reef fishes. It has been suggested that artificial structures can contribute to the dispersal and establishment of the lionfish (*Pterois* spp.). Lionfish, native to the western Pacific, Red Sea, and eastern Indian oceans, were first reported in the 1980s along south Florida and are now well established in the Caribbean and along the Southeast U.S., including the Florida Keys National Marine Sanctuary (Ruiz-Carus et al. 2006, Morris et al. 2009). In July 2011, lionfish were observed for the first time in the Flower Garden Banks National Marine Sanctuary. Lionfish have been observed on eight oil and gas platforms in the Northwestern Gulf of Mexico region. One of these sightings was made on March 24, 2012 on a platform (HI-A-376-A) within 2 nautical miles of the East Flower Garden Bank boundary; it was removed by divers (M. Johnston, FGBNMS, pers. comm. 2012). The remaining platforms in which lionfish were observed are located 125-230 nautical miles east of the sanctuary. In addition, six lionfish were observed and removed on the *Texas Clipper*, a sunken merchant marine vessel approximately 200 nautical miles southwest of the sanctuary, on October 13, 2011 (M. Johnston, FGBNMS, pers. comm. 2011).

The increasing abundance and wider distribution of lionfish in the South Atlantic Bight, Bermuda, Florida, and the Bahamas indicates that lionfish are the first marine fish species in recent times to successfully establish a breeding population in the tropical western Atlantic. Lionfish are ambush predators, and can threaten local ecosystems by altering the structure of native reef fish communities by out-competing local species and reducing forage fish biomass (Morris and Whitfield 2009). Impacts from lionfish could include direct competition with groupers and other carnivores for food, and increased predation on reef fish and crustaceans (Ruiz-Carus et al. 2006, Albins and Hixon 2008, Morris and Akins 2009). Also, lionfish pose a danger to divers and fishermen – stings from the venomous spines of the fish may result in pain, swelling, numbness and sometimes more severe effects including paralysis and systemic effects.

Smith (2006) suggests from research conducted in the Bahamas that lionfish are capable of invading natural patch reefs in the absence of artificial structures, but the presence of artificial reefs facilitates colonization of marginal habitats like sand-seagrass and to a lesser extent, hard bottoms. This pattern suggests that artificial structures represent a resource subsidy to lionfish. Sand-seagrass is marginal habitat for lionfish due to the lack of suitable substrate, but adding artificial structures facilitates lionfish dispersal, thus allowing it to support similar abundances as those found in more structurally complex, higher-quality natural habitats such as on coral reefs and hard bottoms. This pattern has implications for lionfish local persistence and rates of regional spread. Sand-seagrass may naturally function as sink habitats for lionfish in which local populations are maintained by continued migration from more productive sources such as coral reefs. Adding artificial structures may promote a transition from a sink[6] to a source habitat in which the formation of self-sustaining populations allows for the net export of individuals or larvae to new areas.

Smith (2006) also demonstrated that lionfish are slow to colonize artificial reefs, especially in comparison to most native Atlantic fishes, thus suggesting that the rapid range expansion of lionfish in the Atlantic is not due to superior colonizing ability. Therefore, removing or preventing the placement of artificial structures may slow the spread of lionfish, particularly in marginal habitats; however, it is unlikely to prevent their expansion. Instead, their rapid invasion may more likely be linked to their novel predation strategies, unique reproduction, lack of predators, ability to maintain fine-scale positioning in the water column, and superior defense mechanisms.

In order to avoid and/or slow the introduction, establishment, and proliferation of invasive species it has been suggested that resource managers should consider removing or minimizing the addition of submerged artificial structures in coastal and estuarine habitats since they will likely increase the biomass and perhaps the diversity of invasives in these systems (Wasson et al. 2005, Smith 2006, Glasby et al. 2007, Tyrrell and Byers 2007, Sheehy and Vik 2010).

---

[6] In some instances where artificial reefs are popular dive attractions (e.g., regularly visited by dive operators), some dive operators have taken the approach of "adopting" the reef and regularly remove the invasive lionfish. For example, the U.S.S. *Vandenberg*, a submerged vessel in the Florida Keys National Marine Sanctuary, is visited by multiple dive boats each day and lionfish are regularly removed. As a result, the density of lionfish on the U.S.S. *Vandenberg* is significantly lower in comparison to adjacent natural reefs. As anecdotal evidence, one dive master from Dive Key West, Inc. stated that during the lionfish derbies they specifically avoid the public artificial reefs to collect lionfish as time is better spent over natural reefs where lionfish densities are greater. Therefore, it is possible that artificial reefs such as the U.S.S. *Vandenberg* may act as a 'sink' for the local lionfish densities (K. Mille, FWCC, pers. comm., 2012).

## Disease Introduction or Acceleration

Artificial structures may also affect ecosystem function by increasing disease frequency in fish and invertebrates. The normal soft muddy sand bottom of the Gulf of Mexico is considered poor habitat for the dinoflagellate *Gambierdiscus toxicus* that causes ciguatera fish poisoning in humans. However, the elevated hard substrate provided by constructed reefs or platforms supports corals and other components that do provide appropriate substrate. Villareal et al. (2007) reported that the increased availability of hard substrate provided by the oil and gas industry in the Gulf of Mexico has contributed to the proliferation of *G. toxicus*. Constructed reefs are actively used by fishers, providing a connection between fish consumers and potentially toxic fish (Villareal et al. 2007). Although a clear linkage between oil and gas platforms or artificial reefs and ciguatera has not yet been demonstrated, these findings suggest that the provision of reef hard substrate in areas commonly devoid of this habitat may have unintended consequences for human health.

## Toxicological Impacts

Deployment of artificial reefs containing PCBs, heavy metals, oil and fuel residues, and other toxic chemicals could pose a potential risk of contamination to the underwater environment, especially in sensitive coastal ecosystems. Therefore, prior to deployment, structures are typically stripped of potentially hazardous materials in order to make them environmentally safe in accordance with the EPA Best Management Practices for preparing vessels intended to create artificial reefs (EPA MARAD 2006). The removal of petroleum products, hazardous materials, paint cans, batteries, plastics, oil and fuel is specified on the U.S. Coast Guard's Ocean Disposal/Artificial Reef Inspection form. Additionally, under the Toxic Substances Control Act (TSCA), the Environmental Protection Agency (EPA) has the authority to gather data on and regulate chemical substances and mixtures imminently hazardous or presenting an unreasonable risk of injury to public health or the environment. Still some materials of concern below EPA thresholds may potentially remain on vessels permitted to be scuttled as artificial reefs. Such materials include asbestos, polychlorinated biphenyls (PCBs), iron, lead paint, and antifouling paint. As such, biological communities associated with artificial reefs are potentially exposed to pollutants emanating from these structures; therefore, resource managers should consider the risks associated with materials remaining on vessels to be used as artificial reefs (Boland et al. 1983).

Asbestos is the name given to six naturally occurring minerals that are effective as insulators and fire retardants. Its fibers are resistant to heat and chemicals and do not dissolve in water. Asbestos was used in spray-on insulation, ceiling tiles, floor tiles, and fire doors among other things until it was banned in 1989. Friable asbestos, that which is easily crumbled, releasing fibers, is the most hazardous. Sprayed on asbestos is an example of highly friable asbestos. Floor tiles containing asbestos are not highly friable and will release asbestos fibers only when damaged or disturbed. Several studies have investigated the effects of friable asbestos on fish (Batterman and Cook 1981, Belanger et al. 1990, Belanger et al. 1986, Woodhead et al. 1983). Findings indicate that asbestos concentrations on the order of $10^6$ to $10^8$ fibers/L may cause epidermal lesions, epithelial hypertrophy, kidney damage, decreased orientation and swimming ability, degradation of the lateral line, reduced growth, and mortality in fish. Asbestos has also been found to decrease the survival rate of the brine shrimp *Artemia salina* (Stewart and Schurr 1980). Friable asbestos is required to be properly removed and disposed of during the process of preparing an artificial reef. Scientific studies utilizing non-friable asbestos plates and cement to investigate successional patterns of fouling communities and collection of oyster spat, respectively, illustrate the relative harmlessness of undisturbed, non-friable asbestos (Montoya et al. 1985, Garcia and Salzwedel 1995).

PCBs have been used in water-tight gaskets, cable insulations, paints, transformers, capacitors and other components of ex-Navy vessels (Eisler and Belisle 1996). They are lipophilic, highly persistent chemicals. PCBs have been implicated in: reduced primary productivity in phytoplankton; reduced hatchability of contaminated fish and bird eggs; reproductive failure in seals; altered steroid levels and subsequent reproductive impairment in fish and sea stars; reduced fertilization efficiency in sea urchins; and reduced plasma retinol and thyroid hormone levels potentially leading to increased susceptibility to microbial infections, reproductive disorders and other pathological alterations in seals and other marine mammals (Adams and Slaughter-Williams 1988, Brouwer et al. 1989, Clark 1992, den Besten et al. 1991). The Florida Fish and Wildlife Conservation Commission sampled reef fish at Oriskany Reef, a decommissioned former aircraft carrier that was deployed by the U.S. Navy as an artificial reef in May 2006 in the Gulf of Mexico, southeast of Pensacola, FL. The Navy applied for and received a PCB risk-based disposal permit from the EPA (EPA 2005) to allow certain PCB materials to remain onboard vessels based on the results of leachate and toxicological monitoring studies and the conclusions of an independent science advisory board panel (Page 2006, SPARWAR 2006a, b, c, d). The results of the first five years of post-deployment monitoring of reef fish from the Oriskany Reef found a declining trend in PCB levels for sampled reef fish. Initially, and of concern, the mean PCB levels for sampled fish within the first two years of deployment exceeded both the Florida Department of Health (FDOH) and EPA screening values. Between years two and three the PCB level measured decreased to below the FDOH value and slightly above the EPA value. After three years, the mean PCB levels were below both the FDOH and EPA thresholds (Dodrill et al. 2011).

Vessel hulls are typically painted with antifouling paints. Copper and tributyltin (TBT) are the two most common active ingredients in antifouling paints, and typically have an effective life span of five years or less. TBT has been found to be toxic to non-target, non-fouling organisms at ng/L levels and efforts to establish a world-wide ban have been made by the International Maritime Organization since 1998. TBT is banned in many nations and was banned in the U.S. in 1988. Its most marked effects have been the induction of shell thickening and growth anomalies in oysters and imposex (development of sexual organs of the opposite sex) in the dogwhelk (*Nucella lapillus*) potentially leading to sterility. Sterility in *N. lapillus* has been noted at concentrations as low as 3-5 ng Sn/L (approximately 7.5-10.5 ng TBT/L) (Gibbs et al. 1988). Oysters exposed to TBT concentrations >2 ng/L have displayed progressive increases in chambering and at levels

18

above 100 ng TBT/L severely abnormal shell morphology (Laughlin 1996). At higher concentrations (0.5-1.8 g TBT oxide/L), TBT-based paint leachate has been found to elicit polyp retraction, pigmentation loss, and death in corals. The discovery of the highly toxic nature of TBT-based paints has led many countries to ban the use of these paints for non-aluminum hulled vessels less than 25 meters in length. In the case of large steel vessels proposed as artificial reefs, typically by the time artificial reefing is considered as an option the vessels have effectively exceeded their life expectancy and the active ingredients in antifouling paint are no longer effective. Furthermore, the target upright deployment of steel vessels results in the hull being located underneath the ship, and not exposed for epibenthic colonization, assuming deployment occurs as planned (K. Mille, FWCC, pers. comm., 2012).

Heavy metals can be divided into nonessential elements (lead, mercury, and probably cadmium) and essential elements with relatively well-defined roles and functions (copper, iron, selenium, and zinc) (Thompson 1990). In the case of essential metals, body concentrations of metabolically available metal must obtain a minimum concentration (Rainbow 1990). The accumulation of metal in organisms will depend on mechanisms of accumulation and methods of detoxification.

Copper, though an effective antifoulant, has not shown the extensive effects on non-target organisms. At low concentrations, copper is a minor nutrient for both plants and animals involved in biological processes such as oxygen transport and enzyme activity. When present in high concentrations, however, copper can be toxic to aquatic life. In fish, it has been found to cause histological alterations, reduced egg production, abnormalities in newly hatched fry and reduced survival of young (Sorensen 1991).

Steel hulls on vessels scuttled as artificial reefs potentially contribute iron to the marine environment. Iron is an essential component of electron transport in almost all living organisms (Ferreira and Straus 1994). As an essential element, iron levels will tend to be closely regulated by organisms, and thus, it is unlikely that any pollution-derived effects will be observed except in severe and localized cases (Thompson 1990). Corals living in seawater with high concentrations of iron have been found to incorporate the metal into their skeletons (Brown et al. 1991). Elevated iron concentrations have also been found to lead to a loss of zooxanthellae from coral tissues (Harland and Brown 1989). This response is diminished in corals regularly exposed to iron, suggesting corals can alter their accumulation and detoxification pathways to adapt to iron exposure. However, it has also been documented that the unnatural presence of an iron source to an ecosystem can lead to a phase shift in species composition of coral reef ecosystems. For example, the steel hull of a shipwreck in 1991 at the remote Palmyra Atoll in the central Pacific Ocean is believed to be the primary driver behind a phase shift from coral to corallimorpharians (Work et al. 2008). Phase shifts such as this can have long-term negative impacts on coral reefs, and eradication of the organisms responsible for phase shifts in marine ecosystems can be difficult. Therefore, the researchers of this study ultimately suggest that shipwrecks in coral reef ecosystems be immediately removed to mitigate the potential of reef overgrowth by invasives (Work et al. 2008). Studies on phytoplankton and macroalgae indicate that in areas where plant nutrients such as nitrate and phosphate are abundant the availability of iron is actually a limiting factor in growth and biomass (Matsunaga et al. 1994, Wells et al. 1995 Coale et al. 1996, Frost 1996, Takeda 1998). The addition of iron has been seen to increase primary productivity and shift nutrient ratios in such areas. Hence, the concern of unnatural iron inputs from artificial reefs seems not to center on the occurrence of adverse toxicological effects in marine organisms but rather on the alteration of the composition of natural assemblages of algae and species that compete with algae.

Lead based paint was banned in the 1970s and therefore will likely only present as a problem in older ships that have sunk. Lead has no biological function and, therefore, is not metabolized and can accumulate in organisms (Thompson 1990). Corals have been found to incorporate lead into their skeletons (Dodge and Gilbert 1984). In general, marine fish, mammals, and birds exhibit low levels of lead, although bird bones have been shown to concentrate lead compared to other tissues (Thompson 1990). Unicellular algae and sea urchins seem to be the most sensitive marine organisms (Bernhard 1980). Growth inhibition has been observed in the algae species *Thalassiosira pseudonana* and *Porphyridium marinum* exposed to 200 g Pb/L. Sea urchins are sensitive at similar levels.

Oil and gas reserves are frequently located near natural reefs and the reef fish associated with the oil and gas platforms support a significant commercial fishery. It has been suggested that fish can be directly exposed to contaminants from the platform discharges (pollutants come from drilling muds which are frequently discharged from the structures), and therefore, the possibility may also exist for contaminant exposure to humans through consumption of the contaminated fish (Boland et al. 1983). However, a recent study by Love et al. (2009) compared elemental metal concentrations in platform-dwelling fishes to those same species from natural sites, focusing on a large suite of elements likely to be released during platform operations. The natural reefs, which served as reference sites, were located at distances far enough away to be uninfluenced by contaminants originating from platforms. Although there was substantial variability in concentrations of a number of heavy metal elements among fishes, there was no consistent pattern of higher concentrations of any element at either platforms or natural sites. In addition, the study characterized the reproductive capabilities of Pacific sanddabs (*Citharichthys sordidus*, a species of limited home range that remains in close proximity to its reef structure) living around platforms and on natural sites to assess for possible indirect effects of the hypothesized contaminants from platforms on reproduction. The study found no consistent pattern of significantly higher levels of severely atretic eggs among sanddabs from either platform or natural sites (atresia has been widely used as an indicator of pollutant-related reproductive impairment in fishes).

Despite the potential toxicological effects of the chemicals discussed above, adverse effects will not occur unless the chemicals are present at or above their effective concentrations. In 1998, the South Carolina Department of Natural Resources assessed the levels of PCBs and heavy metals in biota found on ex-military ships used as artificial reefs. They collected over 100 samples of reef materials, resident invertebrates, and resident finfish from several locations along the South Carolina coast including permitted artificial reefs and naturally occurring hard bottom reefs. The artificial reef structures selected for the study were primarily ex-military vessels that had been submerged for 3 to 17 years. Three of seven vessels from which biological samples were collected were found to have materials onboard containing PCBs. The PCBs found were in gaskets and cable insulation with concentrations ranging from 1.3 to 24.5 ppm. Of the 80 tissue samples analyzed for PCBs, only 19 (4 finfish, 14 mollusks, and 1 echinoderm) were found above detectable limits. All were well below the U.S. Food and Drug Administration's alert action level of 2.0 ppm wet weight. No significant differences were detected for PCB concentrations in the tissues of organisms collected from vessels found to contain PCB-laden materials, vessels where the presence of PCBs in onboard components was possible but not confirmed, and natural hard bottom control sites. The same tissue samples were also analyzed for metals. Although some individual tissue samples were moderately high in a particular metal, no clear correlation of high metal levels and a particular type of sample site (control versus ship reef) was found. Much higher levels of lead were found in some gastropods removed from artificial reefs when compared to low numbers for bivalves and fish off the same site. The investigators felt the high levels were likely attributable to gastropods grazing directly on the painted surfaces of ships and ingesting minute quantities of lead-rich paint. No indication of bioaccumulation of lead in higher trophic levels was seen. It was concluded that the PCB and metal levels detected in the study did not indicate increased hazards around military ships used as artificial reefs. (Martore et al. 1998)

## Impacts to the Physical and Chemical Attributes of the Ecosystem

Deployment of an artificial reef can also affect the physical and chemical attributes of the ecosystem, which in turn, impacts the living resources of the system. Just as in the ecological dynamics of a natural hard bottom reef community, parameters such as circulation, currents, wave force, and sedimentation affect the diversity and density of living resources that colonize and utilize the structure of artificial reefs. Strong circulation and currents are important in carrying nutrients and organic matter to living resources on artificial reefs. Sedimentation can be harmful to some sessile benthic organisms because sediment particles can smother reef organisms, can clog pores of sponges, inhibit polyp feeding, reduce light available for photosynthesis, and inhibits the exchange of dissolved nutrients and gases. It has been shown that areas of high velocity flow and strong current and low sedimentation correspond to regions of high sessile benthic cover and species diversity, while areas of decelerated flow and increased sedimentation correspond to regions of less cover and lower species diversity. In regards to shipwrecks, the long axis of a wreck, when oriented perpendicular to the prevailing current, typically exhibits areas of higher velocity and energy and lower sedimentation rates, in comparison to midship. As such, these portions of shipwrecks are typically more productive since many of the sessile invertebrates found on these reefs are suspension feeders and obtain nutrients from organic particles and planktonic organisms in the water column (Baynes and Szmant 1989).

The Bureau of Ocean Energy Management (BOEM, formerly part of the Minerals Management Service) has sponsored a series of ecosystem investigations and monitoring studies to better predict, assess, and manage the effect of outer continental shelf oil and gas development activities on marine environments. Their studies assist with understanding the impacts that artificial reefs, in the form of oil and gas platforms, have on the physical and chemical attributes of the ecosystem. They have documented that the presence of a platform or platform group had little effect on ambient water properties (Kennicutt 1995). They did find, however, that alteration of the benthic environment adjacent to offshore platforms resulted from the presence of the platforms, materials discharged from the platforms, and the oceanographic setting. Sediments close to the platforms were highly enriched in sand-sized materials and contaminated with high levels of heavy metals (such as chromium, cadmium, lead, and zinc) that resulted in significant biological responses in some living resources (e.g., sea urchin eggs, polychaetes, copepods). Contaminated sediments were usually confined to within 100 meters of a platform (Kennicutt 1995). However, hydrocarbon concentrations at platforms were low, especially when compared to coastal sediment levels. In addition, PAH concentrations were below levels known to induce biological responses. Also, no enhanced bioaccumulation of contaminants in fish or invertebrates was detected near platforms.

## Longevity and Structural Integrity

The structural integrity, long-term stability and deployment location of artificial reefs can be compromised by environmental impacts such as storm and hurricane damage, waves and high surf, and other harsh environmental conditions. Impacts to artificial reefs can vary greatly and largely depend on the structural design, materials used, age of the artificial reef, geographic location, orientation, and water depth of the artificial reef. As such, impacts from environmental factors can range from no disturbance at all, to some movement, to partial or total structural modification (Blair et al. 1994). Little published literature exists[7] regarding the general longevity and structural integrity of artificial reefs This is likely due to the fact that funding for restoration projects is short-term and there is usually little funding available to monitor and evaluate the long-term success of artificial reefs (E. Marsden, UVM, pers. comm., 2012).

Stability and wave attenuation analyses have been conducted on various models of materials to be used for artificial reefs, including all-concrete, concrete with rubber tire chips, limerock boulders, and Reef Ball[TM] artificial reef units (Zadikoff et al. 1996). All-concrete and limerock boulders were found to be the most stable[8] as individual units and in mound structures. Experimental concrete structures with rubber tire chips were the least stable units.

Brock and Norris (1989) compared the design of four artificial reefs to determine their long-term stability. They found that reefs composed of haphazardly dumped scrap materials (e.g., automobile shells and surplus concrete pipe) were highly unstable and exhibited low life expectancies. Due to their high mass to volume ratio, reefs composed of modules of scrap automobile tires set in concrete bases and dumped haphazardly were relatively stable, but the design precluded effective stacking, resulting in low relief structures. Finally, an artificial reef constructed in an open framework of concrete cube modules had a long life expectancy and stability in high energy environments.

Studies have shown that artificial reefs constructed of high-density, heavily ballasted tires with strong bases show stronger stability in comparison to unballasted tires, which often fail (Myatt et al. 1989, Morley 2009). In 1967 approximately two million unballasted tires were deployed in bundles approximately 1.8 kilometers (km) offshore of Broward County, Florida in 21 meters (m) of water on sandy substrate. Within a few years (some, almost immediately), the bindings on the tire bundles failed and they became mobile with normal currents, and especially during high energy storms (D. E. Britt Assoc. 1974, 1975). As a result of these observations, tire deployments in Florida were ended by the 1980s. The tires have since moved extensively, travelling kilometers from their original

---

[7] Some monitoring reports of artificial reefs document long-term stability and longevity of large concrete and limestone boulders and modules over time (see CPE 2007, Sathe et al. 2010).

[8] Oftentimes, stable artificial structures, such as rocks and prefabricated concrete blocks, are used as a submerged breakwater to provide opportunities for environmental enhancement, aesthetics and wave protection in coastal areas. However, these structures are usually designed and developed from an engineering point of view and do not function as fish habitat or substrata for coral, seaweed, and other living resources (Armono and Hall 2002).

location to beaches and deeper waters offshore. Many of the loose tires have also physically damaged benthic reef fauna on natural reefs. A large-scale removal plan of the tires was initiated in 2001 (Morley 2009). Interestingly, as a result of their continued movement, it has also been shown that tires have the least amount of living resource recruitment in comparison to other materials used for artificial reef construction (Fitzhardinge and Bailey-Brock 1989).

*Hurricane Impacts*

Many studies have examined the impacts severe storms and hurricanes have had on artificial reefs. Hurricane damage to artificial reefs can range from none to moderate to severe and the variance in damage is the result of the size and speed of storms, the frequency of storms, associated wave surges and heights, and local bathymetry and topography.

A study by Bell and Hall (1994) examined the impacts that Hurricane Hugo (Category 4, September 1989) had on a system of nearshore and offshore artificial reefs off the coast of South Carolina. Studies were conducted over a two year period following the storm to assess structural damage, movement of reef materials, environmental effects, and biological impacts. Their results showed that movement of and damage to artificial reef materials was minimal, as only four out of 19 artificial reefs showed major impacts in the form of reef material movement (some movement of small reef structures to a distance of 1.9 km was observed), structural damage, burial or severe subsidence of reef materials. Vessels and PVC reefs showed the greatest impacts. Effects of the storm on artificial reef fish communities as well as resident epibenthic invertebrates were minimal and short term in nature, with no quantifiable detrimental impacts observed. However, water turbidity in the vicinity of many of the nearshore and offshore artificial reefs was dramatically increased for over a year following the storm due to the input of large quantities of estuarine mud into coastal waters.

Damage to artificial reefs in southeastern Florida resulting from Hurricane Andrew (Category 4, August 1992) has also been assessed. Studies have shown that reefs deeper than 43 m were not significantly damaged, however, shallower artificial reefs from 12 – 30 m deep showed a 50% damage rate. The data indicated that the damage was likely the result of wave height and secondarily from storm surge (Coastal Tech 1993). Another study by Blair et al. (1994) assessed the damage resulting from Hurricane Andrew to eleven artificial reefs offshore of Miami-Dade County, Florida. Steel ships, tugs and barges represented 70% of the artificial reefs studied, with 82% of these placed seaward of the outer reef. The remaining 30% of the artificial reefs were composed of other materials including wooden vessels, steel tanks, prefabricated steel tetrahedrons and oil platforms. Blair et al. showed that following Hurricane Andrew 65% of the artificial reefs exhibited some degree of alteration, either via movement, burial, scouring or structural degradation. Alteration to ships, tugs, and barges included movement (from only a few meters up to 457 meters); overturning, bending, cracking and splitting of the vessel; and in some instances, complete loss of structural integrity. In addition, most encrusting organisms (soft corals, sponges, hard corals) were scoured from the surfaces of the

24

artificial structures. Reefs composed of concrete materials had a similar range of alterations. The artificial reefs located within and to the north of the storm's core experienced the greatest structural changes; however, impacts did not exhibit a consistent pattern. One of the five oil platforms in the region was also impacted and suffered numerous broken weld joints, causing the platform to list to the west at a 35 degree angle. Interestingly, numerous instances were noted where a reef was severely modified or moved while an adjacent reef of similar material (e.g., ships of approximately the same size and relief) remained on location or was structurally unchanged. Despite the reefs' new or altered structural configurations, all artificial reef materials remained suitable for recolonization by benthic organisms, and in some instances may have actually improved habitat quality. Another study by Bortone (1992) examined the effects that Hurricane Andrew had on automobiles that had been deployed as artificial reefs off the coast of Pensacola, FL in the northern Gulf of Mexico. Their findings showed that the hurricane resulted in little shifting or movement of the automobiles. Regardless, by 1990, automobiles were prohibited as artificial reef material in Florida.

Studies have demonstrated that some artificial reef materials are more durable and stable when faced with a hurricane. For example, researchers examined the impacts that Hurricanes Erin (Category 2, August 1995) and Opal (Category 3, October 1995) had on over forty artificial reefs located in the northern Gulf of Mexico (Bortone and Turpin 1997, Turpin and Bortone 2002). Materials of higher density were least affected by wave surge, while lighter weight materials were moved distances of at least 1,000 m. Automobiles and steel shipping boxes experienced the most movement as a result of the hurricanes, radio tower sections experienced some movement (anywhere from 90 – 1,000 m), while concrete pilings, pipes, prefabricated reef modules, steel oil rigs, and steel tugboats and barges were found to be the most stable and durable materials. Interestingly, their results also showed that because some artificial reefs were displaced, fishing pressure was greatly reduced for at least one year. As a result of these studies of materials deployed in the 1960s, 70s, and 80s, automobiles, steel shipping boxes, and other lightweight materials have not been deployed in Florida since the 1990s.

Impacts of Hurricane Charley (Category 4, August 2004) to artificial reefs located in Southwest Florida were also examined (Maher 2006). Overall, relatively low levels of impacts to the artificial reef materials were observed on most of the reefs surveyed. However, there was a consistently high level of removal of the majority of invertebrates that had encrusted the structures. It was speculated that the lack of major structural impacts was the result of the very narrow wind swath of the hurricane, as well as the fact that the storm moved very rapidly over the area. Storm-related impacts did vary based on the materials used to construct the reefs and their location. For example, a structural weak steel barge exhibited significant damage, while a stronger steel car ferry did not appear to have been impacted.

Artificial reef structural damage caused by Hurricane Ivan off the coast of Escambia County, FL (Category 3, September 2004) has also been examined. Four materials were studied – fish havens (hollow, floorless concrete three sided units reinforced with metal re-bar), modules designed as "walter modules" (10' x 10' base hollow concrete tetrahedron with metal panels attached to the three sides), Goliath Reef Ball™ (reef balls constructed of granite rock); and hollow concrete Reef Ball™. Following the hurricane, half of the fish havens had collapsed and all that remained were loose piles of irregular concrete pieces. Several of the Walter Modules were damaged with about half showing the steel plate walls torn from the concrete frames. Only one of twenty Goliath Reef Ball™ was broken as a result of the hurricane, while 11% of the standard Reef Ball™ had been damaged due to the hurricane, though it was unknown if the reef balls were previously damaged during the deployment process (Horn and Mille 2004).

*Florida Keys National Marine Sanctuary*

In the Florida Keys National Marine Sanctuary stability issues have arisen on two artificial reefs. In 1998 Hurricane Georges (Category 4, September 1998) broke the sunken vessel *Eagle* in half (J. Delaney, FKNMS, pers. comm., 2012). The U.S.S. *Spiegel Grove*, which was scuttled as an artificial reef in 2002, sank prematurely and settled inverted on the bottom with its bow 11 meters in the air. The vessel remained lying on the her side for nearly three years until Hurricane Dennis (Category 4, July 2005) tipped the vessel to the upright position into a 20 ft hole that had developed beneath the keel as a result of scouring from currents over the previous three years (Farrell and Wood 2009). Interestingly, the resulting upright position of the vessel maintains the same coordinates as prior to Hurricane Dennis at a depth approximately 20 ft deeper in the scour hole, which presumably provides improved long-term stability.

Considering that Florida has the largest number of permitted artificial reef sites in the United States (Mostkoff 1992) it is understandable that the state has contracted the development of software to predict the long term stability of artificial reefs. In 2000, the Florida Fish and Wildlife Commission contracted Paul Lin & Associates, Inc. to develop an Artificial Reef Stability Analysis Software to examine the stability of deployed artificial reef materials under given storm conditions throughout the state (Paul Lin & Associates, Inc. 2000). The software provides models that would allow artificial reef administrators in coastal counties to determine the deployment water depth, orientation, and reef material weight for a proposed artificial reef program. Similarly, in 2001 the Miami-Dade County Department of Environmental Resources Management tasked Coastal Systems International, Inc. with developing computer software that analyzes the behavior of objects that are proposed to be used to create artificial reefs under complex ocean conditions. The software uses historic wave condition data for the entire coast of Florida to predict the forces on and the stability of the proposed reef (DERM 2001). As a result of using these software stability analysis programs, and through evaluation of performance of existing artificial reefs over time, artificial reef deployments since 2000 undergo more scrutiny than the experimental materials of the 1960s-1990s.

*Flower Garden Banks National Marine Sanctuary and the Gulf of Mexico*

Hurricanes Katrina (Category 5, August 2005) and Rita (Category 5, September 2005) were two of the most intense Atlantic hurricanes ever recorded in the Gulf of Mexico and created considerable damage to a wide range of energy infrastructure, shutting down eight refineries, hundreds of oil-drilling and production platforms, and many other industrial facilities (Cruz and Krausmann 2008). These two hurricanes caused the largest number of destroyed and damaged platforms and pipelines, and the highest number of mobile offshore drilling units set adrift in the history of Gulf of Mexico operations (Darby et al. 2006, Cruz and Krausmann 2008). Hurricane Katrina destroyed 44 platforms and severely damaged 21 others (MMS 2006a, b) and Hurricane Rita destroyed 69 platforms and severely damaged 32 others (Djamarani 2005, MMS 2006a). Sixty percent of the platforms that were destroyed were built 30 or more years ago prior to the adoption of more stringent design standards that went into effect in 1977 (Cruz and Krausmann 2008). In addition, many of the platforms that were destroyed were older, smaller producers in relatively shallow waters. Structural damage to platforms included complete toppling of sections and tilting or leaning of platforms. The primary cause for damage to the integrity of platform structures were the loadings caused by wave inundation of the deck (Energo Engineering 2007) (wave inundation increases the horizontal load and overturning moment of the structure resulting in failure and possible collapse).

The shipwreck *Texas Clipper* was intentionally placed in an artificial reef site off the lower Texas coast, approximately 200 nautical miles southwest of the sanctuary, in November 2007. It was substantially damaged by Hurricane Ike (Category 4, September 2008) ten months later. Although the site did not take a direct hit from the storm, which was a Category 1 and 2 storm while in the Gulf of Mexico, a large crack was produced and the stern section of the ship fell to the seafloor. The hurricane made landfall on the upper Texas coast and hurricane strength winds (greater than 74 mph) were not recorded within 150 nautical miles of the *Texas Clipper* reef site.

## Human Use and Economic Impacts

Advocates of the economic benefits of artificial reef development hypothesize that sinking an artificial structure in the vicinity of a natural reef environment can reduce human use pressure on the surrounding natural reefs, increases businesses to local dive operators, and increases economic impact on the local economy (Leeworthy 2011). In Florida, artificial reefs can account for a significant proportion of economic benefit. For example, a study by Johns et al. (2001)[9] found that in 2000 artificial reefs accounted for $117.6 million in expenditures for the Monroe County, Florida economy. In addition, artificial reef related expenditures accounted for 24% of the economic contribution of all reefs, including natural reefs in the county. This study also demonstrated that artificial reefs accounted for $32.5 million in income and approximately 2,300 jobs for the local economy. Additionally, according to this study, there appears to be a very high public demand for artificial reefs in the Florida Keys (the study estimated that annual use values for maintaining existing artificial reefs was $9.4 million, while use value for new artificial reefs was $2.1 million per year. In general, the use value is the maximum amount of money that reef users are willing to pay to maintain the reefs in their existing condition and to add more artificial reefs to the reef system).

---

[9] Note that this study was completed prior to the deployment of the two most highly visited artificial reefs in the Florida Keys – the U.S.S. *Spiegel Grove* (2002) and the U.S.S. *Vandenberg* (2009).

Socioeconomic studies conducted at the U.S.S. *Spiegel Grove* and the U.S.S. *Vandenberg*, both submerged vessels in the Florida Keys National Marine Sanctuary, have further demonstrated that the dive charter industry and the local economies benefit from the introduction of decommissioned ships as artificial reefs. Study results at the U.S.S. *Spiegel Grove*, a 510-foot retired navy ship that was intentionally sunk in the waters off of Key Largo, Florida in June 2002, showed that after deployment recreational use of the surrounding natural reefs decreased, while local dive charter business increased, and the greater local economy grew in terms of both income and employment (Leeworthy et al. 2006). Overall, it has been estimated that the following the sinking of the U.S.S. *Spiegel Grove* the local income increased by $961,800 and the local employment increased by approximately 70 jobs. Also, there was an associated increase of $2.6 million dollars in total recreational expenditures and $2.7 million increase in sales/output for the local economy following the deployment. However, results from a similar study conducted at the U.S.S. *Vandenberg*, a 520-foot retired air force missile tracking ship intentionally sunk in the waters off of Key West, Florida in May 2009, did not support the hypothesis that introducing an artificial reef would reduce use on the surrounding natural reefs. However, the hypotheses that diver operator business would increase as would impacts on the local economy were supported (Leeworthy 2011). Following the deployment of the U.S.S. *Vandenberg* the net changes in total recreational expenditures from the pre- to post-deployment period indicated that there was an increase of $6.5 million in total recreational expenditures, which generated a total impact on sales/output of $7.29 million, about $3.2 million in income, and the creation of 105 new jobs. For the scuba and snorkel businesses of Key West, the number of paying dive customers increased by approximately 49,000, or a 188.9% increase in business in total from the pre-deploy to post deployment time frames. It is important to note that the results of both studies depend heavily upon the attributes of the local economy and existing dive business structure and the marine ecosystem and the artificial reef itself; therefore, the conclusions of these studies may only apply to other locations that have similar attributes. Both studies support the idea that decommissioned ships converted to artificial reefs can be successful in promoting economic development and tourism and also yield a net return on investment.

# Cited Literature

Adams, J.A., and S. Slaughter-Williams. 1988. The effects of PCB's (Aroclors 1254 and 1016) on fertilization and morphology in *Arbacia punctulata*. Water Air Soil Pollut. 38:299-310.

AGSMFC (Atlantic and Gulf States Marine Fisheries Commissions). 2004. Guidelines for marine artificial reef materials, 2nd edition. 205pp.

Albins, M. and M. Hixon. 2008. Invasive Indo-Pacific lionfish *Pterois volitans* reduce recruitment of Atlantic coral-reef fishes. Marine Ecology Progress Series 367:233-238.

Ambrose, R.F. 1994. Mitigating the effects of a coastal power plant on a kelp forest community: rationale and requirements for an artificial reef. Bull. Mar. Sci. 55:694-708.

Armono, H.D. and K.R. Hall. 2002. Wave transmission on submerged breakwaters made of hollow hemispherical shape artificial reefs. Canadian Coastal Conference. Victoria, Canada. 1-13.

Atchison, A.D. 2005. Offshore oil and gas platforms as stepping-stones for expansion of coral communities: a molecular genetic analysis. MS Thesis. Dept. of Oceanography and Coastal Sciences. Louisiana State Univ. 94pp.

Baine, M. 2001. Artificial reefs: a review of their design, application, management and performance. Ocean and Coastal Management 44:241-259.

Batterman, A.L. and P.M. Cook. 1981. Determination of mineral fiber concentrations in fish tissues. Can. J. Fish. Aquat. Sci. 38:952-959.

Baynes, T.W. and A.M. Szmant. 1989. Effect of current on the sessile benthic community structure of an artificial reef. Bull. Mar. Sci. 44(2)-545-566.

Belanger, S.E., K. Schurr, D.A. Allen, A.F. Gohara. 1986. Effects of chrysotile asbestos on coho salmon and green sunfish: evidence of pathological stress. Environ. Res. 39:74-85.

Belanger, S.E., D.S. Cherry, J. Cairns, Jr. 1990. Functional and pathological impairment of Japanese Medaka (*Oryzias latipes*) by long-term asbestos exposure. *Aquat. Toxicol.* 17:133-154.

Bell, M. and J.W. Hall. 1994. Effects of Hurricane Hugo on South Carolina's marine artificial reefs. Bull. Mar. Sci. 55(2-3):836-847.

Bernhard, M. 1980. The relative importance of lead as a marine pollutant. *In*: M. Branica and A. Konrad (eds.) Lead in the Marine Environment. Pergamon Press, Elmsford, NY, 345-352.

Blair, S.M., T.L. McIntosh, B.J. Mostkoff. 1994. Impacts of Hurricane Andrew on the offshore reef systems of central and northern Dade County, Florida. Bull. Mar. Sci. 54(3):961-973.

BOEM (United States Department of the Interior Bureau of Ocean Energy Management, Regulation and Enforcement, Gulf of Mexico OCS Region). 2010. Notice to lessees and operators of federal oil and gas leases and pipeline right-of-way holders in the outer continental shelf, Gulf of Mexico region. NTL No. 2010-G05. 11pp.

Bohnsack, J.A. and F. H. Talbot. 1980. Species-packing by reef fishes on Australian and Caribbean reefs: an experimental approach. Bull. Mar. Sci. 30:710-723.

Bohnsack, J.A. and D.L. Sutherland. 1985. Artificial reef research: a review with recommendations for future priorities. Bull. Mar. Sci. 37(1):11-39.

Bohnsack, J.A. 1989. Are high densities of fishes at artificial reefs the result of habitat limitation or behavioral preference? Bull. Mar. Sci. 44:631-645.

Bohnsack, J.A., D.L. Johnson, R.F. Ambrose. 1991. Ecology of artificial reef habitats and fishes. *In*: Artificial Habitats for Marine and Freshwater Fisheries. Academic Press, Inc., pp. 61-107.

Bohnsack, J.A., D.E. Harper, D.B. McClellan, M. Hulsbeck. 1994. Effects of reef size on colonization and assemblage structure of fishes at artificial reefs off southeastern Florida, U.S.A. Bull. Mar. Sci. 55:796-823.

Bohnsack, J.A., A-M, Ecklund, A.M. Szmant. 1997. Essay: artificial reef research: is there more than the attraction-production issue? Fisheries 22:14-16.

Boland, G.S., B.J. Gallaway, J.S. Baker, G.S. Lewbel. 1983. Ecological effects of energy development on reef fish of the Flower Garden Banks. LGL Ecological Research Associates, Inc. 499pp.

Booth, D.J. and D.M. Brosnan. 1995. The role of recruitment dynamics in rocky shore and coral reef fish communities. Av. Ecol. Res. 26:309-385.

Bortone, S.A. 1992. Stability of automobile and helicopter bodies in the northern Gulf of Mexico. University of West Florida. Report submitted to Florida Department of Natural Resources. 20pp.

Bortone, S.A. and R.K. Turpin. 1997. An evaluation of artificial reefs after the influences of hurricanes and fishing pressure. Project no. OFMAS-062. University of West Florida. Report submitted to Santa Rosa County and Florida Department of Environmental Protection. 74pp.

Bortone, S.A. 2008. Coupling fisherieswith ecology through marine artificial reef deployments. Pages 917–924. *In*: J. Nielsen, J. J. Dodson, K. Friedland, T. R. Hamon, J. Musick, E. Verspoor (eds.). Reconciling fisheries with conservation: symposium 49. Proceedings of the fourth world fisheries congress. American Fisheries Society. Bethesda, Maryland.

Brock, R.E. and J.E. Norris. 1989. An analysis of the efficacy of four artificial reef designs in tropical waters. Bull. Mar. Sci. 44(2):934-941.

Brouwer, A., P.J.H. Reijnders, J.H. Koeman. 1989. Polychlorinated biphenyl (PCB)-contaminated fish induces vitamin A and thyroid hormone deficiency in the common seal (*Phoca vitulina*). Aquat. Toxicol. 15:99-106.

Brown, B.E., A.W. Tudhope, M.D.A. Le Tissier, T.P. Scoffin. 1991. A novel mechanism for iron incorporation into coral skeletons. Coral Reefs 10:211-215.

Cairns, S. 2000. A revision of the shallow-water azooxanthellate Scleractinia of the Western Atlantic. Stud Nat Hist Carib 75:1–240.

Carr, M.H. and M.A. Hixon. 1997. Artificial reefs: the importance of comparisons with natural reefs. Fisheries 22(4):28-33.

Caselle, J. E., M.S. Love, C. Fusaro, D. Schroeder. 2002. Trash or habitat? Fish assemblages on offshore oilfield seafloor debris in the Santa Barbara Channel, California. ICES Journal of Marine Science 59:S258–S265.

Clark, R.B. 1992. Marine Pollution. Clarendon Press, Oxford, 172 pp.

Clavero, M. and E. García-Berthou. 2005. Invasive species are a leading cause of animal extinctions. Trends in Ecology and Evolution 20:110.

Coale, K.H., S.E. Fitzwater, R.M. Gordon, K.S. Johnson, R.T. Barber. 1996. Control of community growth and export production by upwelled iron in the equatorial Pacific Ocean. Lett. Nature 379:621-624.

Coastal Tech. 1993. Effects of hurricane Andrews on Dade County's artificial reefs, Florida. Report submitted to Metropolitan Dade County Department of Environmental Resources Management, Miami, Florida 11pp.

Cowan, J.H., C.B. Grimes, W.F. Patterson III, C.J. Walters, A.C. Jones, W.J. Lindberg, D.J. Sheehy, W.E. Pine III, J.E. Powers, M.D. Campbell, K.C. Lindeman, S.L. Diamond, R. Hilborn, H.T. Gibson, K.A. Rose. 2010. Red snapper management in the Gulf of Mexico: science- or faith-based? Rev Fish Biol Fisheries. 18pp.

CPE (Coastal Planning & Engineering, Inc.). 2007. As-built survey of artificial reefs constructed by Pinellas County, Florida; under FDEP permit no. 52-2923209. Prepared for Department of Environmental Management, Pinellas County, Florida. 30pp.

Creed, J.C. 2006. Two invasive alien azooxanthellate corals, *Tubastraea coccinea* and *Tubastraea tagusensis*, dominate the native zooxanthellate *Mussismilia hispida* in Brazil. Coral Reefs 25:350.

Cruz, A.M. and E. Krausmann. 2008. Damage to offshore oil and gas facilities following hurricanes Katrina and Rita: An overview. Journal of Loss Prevention in the Process Industries 21(6)620-626.

Darby, K.A., D.E. Dismukes, S.E. Cureington. Hurricanes and energy infrastructure in the Gulf of Mexico: impacts and challenges. GCAGS Annual Convention Lafayette, Louisiana.

D. E. Britt Associates, Inc. 1974. Report of investigation of Broward artificial reef (tire reef). Report to Broward County Waste Collection & Disposal Division of Solid Waste. 10pp.

D. E. Britt Associates, Inc. 1975. Annual report of investigations of Borward artificial reef (tire reef). Report to Broward County Waste Collection & Disposal Division of Solid Waste. 5pp.

DeMartini, E.E., D.A. Roberts, T.W. Anderson. 1989. Contrasting patterns of fish density and abundance at an artificial rock reef and a cobble-bottom kelp forest. Bull. Mar. Sci. 44:881-892.

den Besten, P.J., J.M.L. Elenbaas, J.R. Maas, S.J. Dieleman, H.J. Herwig, P.A. Voogt. 1991. Effects of cadmium and polychlorinated biphenyls (Clophen A50) on steroid metabolism and cytochrome P-450 monooxygenase system in the sea star *Asterias rubens L*. Aquat. Toxicol. 20:95-110.

DERM (Miami-Dade County Department of Environmental Resources Management). 2001. Artificial reef stability program, version 1.0 documentation. 9pp.

Djamarani, M. 2005. The stakes are rising. Petroleum Review, December.

Dodge, R.E. and T.R. Gilbert. 1984. Chronology of lead pollution contained in banded coral skeletons. Mar. Biol. 82:9-13.

Doherty, P.J. and D.M. Williams. 1988. The replenishment of coral reef fish populations. Oceanogr. Mar. Biol. Annu. Rev. 26:487-551.

Doherty, P.J. and A. Fowler. 1994. Demographic consequences of variable recruitment to coral reef fish populations: a congeneric comparison of two damselfishes. Bull. Mar. Sci. 54:297-313.

Dodrill, J., K. Mille, B. Horn, R. Turpin. 2011. Progress report summarizing the reef fish sampling, PCB analysis results and visual monitoring associated with the Oriskany Reef, a decommissioned former Navy aircraft sunk in 2006 as an artificial reef in the Northeastern Gulf of Mexico off Pensacola, Florida. Florida Fish and Wildlife Conservation Commission, Florida Artificial Reef Program. 136pp.

Eisler, R. and A.A. Belisle. 1996. Planar PCB hazards of fish, wildlife, and invertebrates: a synoptic review. National Biological Service, Biological Report 31, 75 pp.

Eklund, A.M. 1996. The effects of post-settlement predation and resource limitation on reef fish assemblages. Doctoral dissertation, University of Miami, Coral Gables, FL.

Emery, B.M., L. Washburn, M.S. Love, M.M. Mishimoto, J.C. Ohlmann. 2006. Do oil and gas platforms off California reduce recruitment of bocaccio (*Sebastes paucispinis*) to natural habitat? An analysis based on trajectories derived from high-frequency radar. Fish. Bull. 104:391-400.

Energo Engineering. 2007. Assessment of fixed offshore platform performance in hurricanes Katrina and Rita, Final report, Energo Engineering.

EPA (U.S. Environmental Protection Agency). 2005. EPA Science Advisory Board (SAB) Consultation on the Polychlorinated Biphenyl-Artificial Reef Risk Assessment. Letter to the Honorable Stephen L. Johnson, EPA Administrator. EPA-SAB-CON-06-001.

EPA MARAD (U.S. Environmental Protection Agency and U.S. Maritime Administration). 2006. National guidance: best management practices for preparing vessels intended to create artificial reefs. 77pp.

ESA PWA. 2012. Evaluation of erosion mitigation alternatives for Southern Monterey Bay. Prepared for Monterey Bay Sanctuary Foundation and The Southern Monterey Bay Coastal Erosion Working Group. 203pp.

Fager, E.W. 1971. Pattern in the development of a marine community. Limnol. Oceanogr. 16:241-253.

Farrell, J. and S. Wood. 2009. An automated purge valve for marine salvage. IEEE Conference Publishing. 10pp.

Fenner, D. and K. Banks. 2004. Orange cup coral *Tubastraea coccinea* invades Florida and the Flower Garden Banks, Northwestern Gulf of Mexico. Coral Reefs 23:505-507.

Ferreira, F. and N.A. Straus. 1994. Iron deprivation in cyanobacteria. J. Appl. Phycol. 6:199-210.

Ferry, R. 2009. Range expansion of an invasive coral species into South Florida and the Florida Keys National Marine Sanctuary: investigating the ecological impact and source of the invasion. Wetlands, Coastal and Oceans Branch, EPA, Region 4. 6pp.

Fitzhardinge, R.C. and J.H. Bailey-Brock. 1989. Colonization of artificial reef materials by coral and other sessile organisms. Bull. Mar. Sci. 44(2):567-579.

Frost, B.W. 1996. Phytoplankton bloom on iron rations. Nature 383:475-476.

Garcia, C.B. and H. Salzwedel. 1995. Successional patterns on fouling plates in the Bay of Santa Marta, Colombian Caribbean. An. Inst. Invest. Mar. Punta de Betin. 24:95-121.

Gibbs, P.E., P.L. Pascoe, G.R. Burt. 1988. Sex change in the female dog-whelk, *Nucella lapillus*, induced by tributyltin from antifouling paints. J. Mar. Biol. Ass. U.K. 68:715-731.

Glasby, T.M., S.D Connell, M.G. Holloway, C.L. Hewitt. 2007. Nonindigenous biota on artificial structures: could habitat creation facilitate biological invasions? Mar. Biol. 151:887-895.

Grossman, G.D., G.P. Jones, W.J. Seaman. 1997. Do artificial reefs increase regional fish production? A review of existing data. Fisheries 22:17-23.

Harland, A.D, and B.E. Brown. 1989. Metal tolerance in the scleractinian coral *Porites lutea*. Mar. Pollut. Bull. 20:353-357.

Herlan, J. and D. Lirman. 2008. Development of a coral nursery program for the threatened coral *Acropora cervicornis* in Florida. Session number 24. Proceedings of the 11th International Coral Reef Symposium, Ft. Lauderdale, Florida.

Herrnkind, W.F., M.J. Butler IV, J.H. Hunt. 1997. Case study: can artificial habitats that mimic natural structures enhance recruitment of Caribbean spiny lobster? Fisheries 22:24-27.

Hickerson, E.L. and Schmahl, G.P. 2005. The state of coral reef ecosystems in the Flower Garden Banks, Stetson Bank, and Other Banks in the Northwest Gulf of Mexico. Flower Garden Banks National Marine Sanctuary NOAA, pp. 201–221 (Chapter 8).

Horn, B. and K. Mille. 2004. Post hurricane dive assessment of four concrete modular artificial reefs south of Pensacola, FL. Florida Fish and Wildlife Conservation Commission. 20pp.

Johns, G.M., V.R. Leeworthy, F.W. Bell, M.A. Bonn. 2001. Socioeconomic study of reefs in Southeast Florida. Final Report for Broward County, Palm Beach County, Miami-Dade County, Monroe County, Florida Fish and Wildlife Conservation Commission, National Oceanic and Atmospheric Administration. 348pp.

Kennicutt, M.A., II (ed). 1995. Gulf of Mexico offshore operations monitoring experiment, phase I: sublethal responses to contaminant exposure. Final Report. OCS Study MMS 95-0045. U.S. Department of the Interior, Minerals Management Service, Gulf of Mexico OCS Region, New Orleans, Louisiana. 709pp.

Laughlin, R.B. 1996. Bioaccumulation of TBT by aquatic organisms. *In*: M.A. Champ and P.F. Seligman (eds.), Organotin: environmental fate and effects. Chapman and Hall, NY, pp. 331-355.

Leeworthy, V.R., T. Maher, E.A. Stone. 2006. Can artificial reefs alter user pressure on adjacent natural reefs? Bull. Mar. Sci. 78(1):29-37.

Leeworthy, V.R. 2011. The Economic Impact of the U.S.S. *Vandenberg* on the Monroe County Economy. Silver Spring, MD: Office of National Marine Sanctuaries, National Ocean Service, National Oceanic and Atmospheric Administration. 16pp.

Lewbel., G.S., R.L. Howard, B.J. Gallaway. 1987. Zonation of dominant fouling organisms on northern Gulf of Mexico petroleum platforms. Mar. Environ. Res. 21(3):199-224.

LGL Ecological Research Associates. 1998. Cumulative ecological significance of oil and gas structures in the Gulf of Mexico: Information search, synthesis and ecological modeling; Phase 1 Final Report. USGS/BRD/CR - 1997-0006; OCS Study MMS 97-0036. 132pp.

Lindberg, W.J. 1997. Essay: can science resolve the attraction-production issue? Fisheries 22:10-13.

Lindberg, W.J., T.K. Frazer, K.M. Portier, V. Frederic, J. Logtin, D.J. Murie, D.M. Mason, B. Nagy, M.K. Hart. 2006. Density-dependent habitat selection and performance by a large mobile reef fish. Ecological Applications 16(2)731-746.

Love, M.S. and A. York. 2005. A comparison of the fish assemblages associated with an oil/gas pipeline and adjacent seafloor in the Santa Barbara Channel, Southern California. Bull. Mar. Sci. 77(1):101–117.

Love, M.S., D.M. Schroeder, W. Lenarz, A. MacCall, A.S. Bull, L. Thorsteinson. 2006. Potential use of offshore marine structures in rebuilding an overfished rockfish species, bocaccio (*Sebastes paucispinis*). Fisheries Bulletin 104:383-390.

Love, M.S., E. Brothers, D.M. Schroeder, W.H. Lenarz. 2007. Ecological performance of young-of-the-year blue rockfish (*Sebastes mystinus*) associated with oil platforms and natural reefs in California as measured by daily growth rates. Bull. Mar. Sci. 80(1):147-157.

Love, M.S., M. Nishimoto, M. Saiki. 2009. Reproductive ecology and body burden of resident fish prior to decommissioning. OCS Study MMS 2009-019. U.S. Department of the Interior, Minerals Management Service, Pacific Outer Continental Shelf Region. 93pp.

MacArthur, R.H. and E.O. Wilson. 1967. The Theory of Island Biogeography. Princeton University Press.

Maher, T. 2006. Assessment of Hurricane Charley impacts on Southwest Florida artificial reefs. The reef ball foundation. 42pp.

Martore, R.M., T.D. Mathews, M. Bell. 1998. Levels of PCBs and heavy metals in biota found on ex-military ships used as artificial reefs. Marine Resources Division, South Carolina Marine Resources Center, South Carolina Department of Natural Resources, Charleston, SC, unpublished.

Matsunaga, K., Y. Suzuki, K. Kuma, I. Kudo. 1994. Diffusion of Fe(II) from an iron propagation cage and its effect on tissue iron and pigments of macroalgae on the cage. J. Appl. Phycol. 6:397-403.

Meier, M.H., R. Buckley, J.J. Polovina. 1989. A debate on responsible artificial reef development. Bull. Mar. Sci. 44:1051-1057.

Menge, B.A. 1976. Organization of the New England Rocky intertidal community: role of predation, competition, and environmental heterogeneity. Ecological Monographs 46:355-393.

MMS (Minerals Management Service). 2006a. Impact assessment of offshore facilities from Hurricanes Katrina and Rita, News Release 3418, 19 January.

MMS (Minerals Management Service). 2006b. MMS updates hurricanes Katrina and Rita damage, Minerals Management Service, News Release 3486, 1 May.

Montoya, A.J., Q.R. Quesada, Z.E. Madriz, M.E. Castro, P.O. Urpi. 1985. Comparative analysis of substrates for collection of mangrove oyster (*Crassostrea rhizophorae*, Guilding 1828) spat in Viscaya estuary, Limon, Costa Rica. Rev. Biol. Trop. 33:1-6.

Mostkoff, B.J. 1992. Preliminary report: Dade County DERM artificial reef program, the effects of Hurricane Andrew. 10pp.

Morley, D.M. 2009. Environmental enhancement gone awry: characterization of an artificial reef constructed from waste vehicle tires. Masters thesis. NOVA Southeastern University Oceanographic Center. 70pp.

Morris, J.A., Jr. and J.L. Akins. 2009. Feeding ecology of invasive lionfish (*Pterois volitans*) in the Bahamian archipelago. Environmental Biology of Fishes, DOI 10.1007/s10641-009-9538-8.

Morris, J.A., Jr. and P.E. Whitfield. 2009. Biology, ecology, control and management of the invasive Indo-Pacific lionfish: an updated integrated assessment. NOAATechnical Memorandum NOS NCCOS 99. 57pp.

Morris, J.A., Jr., J.L. Akins, A. Barse, D. Cerino, D.W. Freshwater, S.J. Green, R.C. Munoz, C. Paris, P.E. Whitfield. 2009. Biology and ecology of the invasive lionfishes, *Pterois miles* and *Pterois volitans*. Proceedings of the 61st Gulf and Caribbean Fisheries Institute November 10 - 14, 2008 Gosier, Goudeloupe, French West Indies. 6pp.

Myatt, D.O., E.N. Myatt, W.K. Figley. 1989. New Jersey tire reef stability study. Bull. Mar. Sci. 44(2):807-817.

Olden, J.D., N.L. Poff, M.R. Douglas, M.E. Douglas, K.D. Fausch. 2004. Ecological and evolutionary consequences of biotic homogenization. Trends in Ecology and Evolution 19:18–24.

Osenberg, C.W., C.M. St. Mary, J.A. Wilson, W.J. Lindberg. 2002. A quantitative framework to evaluate the attraction-production controversy. ICES J. Mar. Sci., 59: S214–S221.

OST (California Ocean Science Trust). 2010. Executive summary. Evaluating alternatives for decommissioning California's offshore oil and gas platforms. A technical analysis to inform state policy. 18pp.

Otake, S. and M. Oshitani. 2006. Macro-evaluation of catch data from artificial reefs deployed in the Japan Sea. Bull. Mar. Sci. 78(10)221-226.

Pape, T.L. 2006. Polychlorinated biphenyls (PCB) source term estimates for ex-ORISKANY (CVA-34). Fairfax, Virginia, Program Executive Office (Ships); CACI International Inc. and Subsidary Companies: 1-21.

Pattengill, C.V. 1998. The Structure and Persistence of Reef Fish Assemblages of the Flower Garden Banks National Marine Sanctuary. Ph.D. Dissertation. Texas A&M University, College Station, Texas. 164 pp.

Patterson III, W.F., D.T. Addis, M.A. Dance. 2009. The Refuge Effect of Unpublished Artificial Reefs Deployed on the Northwest Florida Shelf (FWC-06120): 2005-08 Modeling Report. Pensacola, FL, University of West Florida: 53pp.

Paul Lin & Associates, Inc. 2000. Artificial reef stability analysis software. Submitted to Florida Fish and Wildlife Conservation Commission and Lee County Department of Environmental Services. 14pp.

Pickering, H. and D. Whitmarsh. 1996. Artificial reefs and fisheries exploitation: a review of the "attraction versus production" debate, the influence of design and its significance for policy. CEMARE Res. Pap., University of Portsmouth, Portsmouth, no.107, 28 pp.

Potts, T.A. and A.W. Hulbert. 1994. Structural influences of artificial and natural habitats on fish aggregations in Onslow Bay, North Carolina. Bull. Mar. Sci. 55:609-622.

Proserv Offshore. 2010. Decommissioning cost update for removing Pacific OCS region offshore oil and gas facilities, January 2010, Volume 1. A Study for the U.S. Department of the Interior, Minerals Management Service. 83pp.

REEF (Reef Environmental Education Foundation). 2007. Fish monitoring on the *Spiegel Grove* artificial reef April 2002 – August 2007 final report. 20pp.
Quinn, T.P. 2009. The influence of artificial reef associated fish assemblages and varying substrates on coral recruitment. Thesis. Nova Southeastern University, Fort Lauderdale-Davie, Florida. 124pp.

Rainbow, P.S. 1990. Heavy metal levels in marine invertebrates. *In*: R.W. Furness and P.S. Rainbow (eds.), Heavy metals in the marine environment. CRC Press, Inc., Boca Raton, pp. 67-79.

Randall, J. E. 1963. An analysis of the fish populations of artificial and natural reefs in the Virgin Islands. Carib. J. Sci. 3:31-47.

Rooker, J.R., G.J. Holt, C.V. Pattengill, Q. Dokken. 1997. Fish assemblages on artificial and natural reefs in the Flower Garden Banks National Marine Sanctuary, USA. Coral Reefs 16:83-92.

Ruiz-Carus, R., R.E. Matheson, D.E. Roberts, P.E. Whitfield. 2006. The western Pacific red lionfish, *Pterois volitans* (Scorpaenidae). *In*: Florida: Evidence for reproduction and parasitism in the first exotic marine fish established in state waters. Biol. Conserv. 128(March):384-390.

Salcido, R.E. 2005. Enduring optimism: examining the rig-to-reef bargain. Ecology Law Quartery 32(863).

Sammarco, P.W., A.D. Atchison, G.S. Boland. 2004. Expansion of coral communities within the northern Gulf of Mexico via offshore oil and gas platforms. Mar. Ecol. Prog. Ser. 260:129–143.

Sathe, M.P, S.E. Thanner, S.M. Blair. 2010. Bal Harbour mitigation artificial reef monitoring program year 10 progress report and summary. Submitted to the State of Florida Department of Environmental Protection in partial fulfillment of the Bal Harbour consent order – OGC Case No. 94-2842. 39pp.

Scarborough-Bull, A., M.S. Love, D.M. Schroeder. 2008. Artificial reefs as fishery conservation tools: contrasting the roles of offshore structures between the Gulf of Mexico and the Southern California Bight. American Fisheries Society, Proceedings of the 4th World Fishery Congress, Vancouver, Canada, pp. 587-603

Schroeder, D.M. and M.S. Love. 2004. Ecological and political issues surrounding decommissioning of offshore oil facilities in the Southern California Bight. Ocean & Coastal Management 47:21–48.

Schmahl, G.P., E.L. Hickerson, W.F. Precht, 2008. Biology and ecology of coral reefs and coral communities in the Flower Garden Banks Region, Northwestern Gulf of Mexico. In, B.M. Riegl and R.E. Dodge, Coral Reefs of the USA, Springer Science, 2008.

Shearer, T. 2010. Distribution of *Tubastraea coccinea* in Florida and Flower Garden Banks: Progress Report. Georgia Institute of Technology. 14pp.

Sheehy, D.J. and S.F. Vik. 1992. Developing prefabricated reefs: an ecological engineering approach. *In*: Thayer, G.W. (ed.), NOAA Symposium on Habitat Restoration. Restoring the Nation's Marine Environment. Maryland Sea Grant, College Park, MD.

Sheehy, D. and S.F. Vik. 2010. The role of constructed reefs in non-indigenous species introductions and range expansions. Ecological Engineering 36:1-11.

Shinn, E.A. 1974. Oil structures as artificial reefs. *In*: Colunga, L. and R. Stone (eds.) Proceedings of an International Conference on Artificial Reefs, March 1974. Houston, TX. TAMU-SG-74-103. pp. 91-96.

Shipp, R. L. 1999. The artificial reef debate: Are we asking the wrong questions? Gulf Mexico Sci., 17(1):51–55.

Shipp, R.L. and S.A. Bortone. 2009. A perspective of the importance of artificial habitat on the management of red snapper in the Gulf of Mexico. Reviews in Fisheries Science 17(1):41-47.

Smith, G.B., D.A. Hensley, H.H. Mathews. 1979. Comparative efficacy of artificial and natural Gulf of Mexico reefs as fish attractants. Fla. Mar. Res. Pub. 35. 7pp.

Smith, N.S. 2006. Lionfish invasion in nearshore waters of the Bahamas: an examination of the effects of artificial structures and invader versus native species colonization rates. Thesis. University of British Columbia, Vancouver. 93pp.

Sorensen, E.M. 1991. Metal poisoning in fish. CRC Press, Inc., Boca Raton, 374 pp.

SPARWAR Systems Center San Diego. 2006a. Artificial reefing: ex-Oriskany artificial reef project - prospective risk assessment model (PRAM) Version 1.4C. San Diego, California. (Prepared for: Program Executiv Office Ships (PMS 333)), Navy Environmental Health Center, URS Corporation, SPARWAR Systems Center, : Sections 1-2, Tables 1-11, Figures 1-15, Appendices A-K.

SPARWAR Systems Center San Diego. 2006b. Ex-Oriskany artificial reef project: human health risk assessment. [Prepared for: Program Executive Office Ships (PMS 333)]: x, Sections 1-11, Appendices A-K.

SPARWAR Systems Center San Diego. 2006c. Ex-Oriskany project: time dynamic model documentation (TDM), [Prepared for: Program Executive Office Ships (PMS 333)]: Section 1, Appendicies A-D.

SPARWAR Systems Center San Diego. 2006d. Ex-Oriskany project: investigation of polychlorinated biphenyl (PCB) release-rates from selected shipboard materials under laboratory-simulated shallow ocean (artificial reef) environments: xvii, 1-219, Appendices pp. 1-836.

Spieler, R.E., D.S. Gilliam, R.L. Sherman. 2001. Artificial substrate and coral reef restoration: what do we need to know to know what we need? Bull. Mar. Sci. 69:1013-1030.

Stewart, S. and K. Schurr. 1980. Effects of asbestos on survival of *Artemia*. Proceedings of the International Symposium on the Brine Shrimp *Artemia salina*. pp. 233-251.

Takeda, S. 1998. Influence of iron availability on nutrient consumption ratio of diatoms in oceanic waters. Nature 393:774-777.

Thompson, D.R. 1990. Metal levels in marine vertebrates. *In:* R.W. Furness and P.S. Rainbow (eds.), Heavy Metals in the Marine Environment. CRC Press, Inc., Boca Raton, pp. 143-182.

Turpin, R.K. and S.A. Bortone. 2002. Pre- and post-hurricane assessment of artificial reefs: evidence for potential use as refugia in a fishery management strategy. ICES Journal of Marine Science 59(S74-S82).

Tyrrell, M.C. and J.E. Byers. 2007. Do artificial substrates favor nonindigenous fouling species over native species? Journal of Experimental Marine Biology and Ecology 342:54-60.

Villareal, T.A., S. Hanson, S. Qualia, E.I.E. Jester, H.R. Granade, R.W. Dickey. 2007. Petroleum production platforms as sites for the expansion of ciguatera in the northwestern Gulf of Mexico. Harmful Algae 6(2):253–259.

Walton, J.M. 1982. The effects of an artificial reef on resident flatfish populations. Mar. Fish. Rev. 44(6-7):45-48.

Wasson, K., K. Fenn, J.S. Pearse. 2005. Habitat differences in marine invasions of central California. Biol. Invasions 7(6):935–948.

Wells, M.L., N.M. Price, K.W. Bruland. 1995. Iron chemistry in seawater and its relationship to phytoplankton: a workshop report. Mar. Chem. 48:157-182.

Woodhead, A.D., R.B. Setlow, V. Pond. 1983. The effects of chronic exposure to asbestos fibers in the Amazon molly, *Poecelia formosa*. Environ. International 9:173-176.

Work, T.M., G.S. Aeby, J.E. Maragos. 2008. Phase shift from a coral to a corallimorph-dominated reed associated with a shipwreck on Palmyra Atoll. PLoS ONE 3(8):e2989.

Zadikoff, G., L. D.M. Covello, Harris, B, Macmillan. 1996. Stability and wave attenuation analyses for concrete and concrete/rubber tetrahedron modules for submerged structures. Shelby and Associates and Florida Institute of Technology. Submitted to City of Miami Beach. 64pp.

# Acknowledgements

Thanks is given to Paula (Souik) Bizot who, in 1998, drafted a white paper for the NOAA Sanctuaries and Reserve Division titled *Considerations for Artificial Reef Development*. Portions of that document were used during the drafting stages of this updated report on the same topic.

This report also benefited significantly from the following individuals who either provided a preliminary review of the report or contributed comments, content, or literature: Greg Boland (Bureau of Ocean Energy Management), Erica Burton (NOAA MBNMS), Thomas Coon (Michigan State University), Brad Damitz (NOAA GFNMS), Natalie Dingledine (DLZ Michigan), Jon Dodrill (FFWCC), Scott Donahue (NOAA FKNMS), Steve Gittings (NOAA ONMS), Kaitlin Graiff (NOAA CBNMS), Russ Green (NOAA TBNMS), Lauren Heesemann (NOAA MNMS), Emma Hickerson (NOAA FGBNMS), Rebecca Holyoke (NOAA ONMS), Hoku Johnson (detail to NOAA ONMS), Michelle Johnston (NOAA FGBNMS), Irina Kogan (formerly of NOAA GFNMS), Vernon R. Leeworthy (NOAA ONMS), Ellen Marsden (University of Vermont), Keith Mille (FFWCC), Michael Murphy (California Coastkeeper Alliance), Steve Rohmann (NOAA ONMS), Jan Roletto (NOAA GFNMS), George Schmahl (NOAA FGBNMS), and Vicki Wedell (NOAA ONMS).

Special thanks is given to Joanne Delaney (NOAA FKNMS), John Embesi (NOAA FGBNMS), and Dale Roberts (NOAA CBNMS) who were particularly helpful in generating content, reviewing and editing text, answering questions, and providing references for this report.

Finally, sincere thanks is also extended to the peer reviewers of this document: Dr. Jim Bohnsack (NOAA National Marine Fisheries Service Southeast Fisheries Science Center), Dr. Ann Scarborough Bull (Environmental Sciences Section, Pacific Region Office of Environment Bureau of Ocean Energy Management), and Mr. Keith Mille (Division of Marine Fisheries - Artificial Reef Program, Fish and Wildlife Conservation Commission).

www.ingramcontent.com/pod-product-compliance
Lightning Source LLC
Chambersburg PA
CBHW080344290526
45791CB00009BA/2730